A Vedic Science Primer

A Vedic Science Primer

Dr. P.S.R. Murthy
Formerly Principal and Dean (Retd).
Osmania University College of Engineering

BSP BS Publications
4-4-309, Giriraj Lane, Sultan Bazar,
Hyderabad - 500 095 A.P.
Phone : 040 - 23445605, 23445688

Published by:

BSP BS Publications
4-4-309, Giriraj Lane, Sultan Bazar, Hyderabad - 500 095 -A.P.
Phone : 040 – 23445605, 23445688; Fax : 91+40-23445611
e-mail : contactus@bspublications.net
website : www.bspublications.net

Printed at

Adithya Art Printers
Hyderabad.

Price : Rs. 125.00

ISBN : 978-81-7800-198-2

Dedicated to

Sanathana Dharma

Acknowledgement

I sincerely acknowledge the great support given to me by Sri K.T. Mahi, Secretary Sree Educational Society and Sri P. Narasimha Reddy, Director, Sreenidhi Institute of Science and Technology, without which I would not have been able to write this book.

My thanks to my wife Nirmala Devi for giving a patient hearing at the manuscript stage and for her constant encouragement.

I thank Sri M.V.L Narasimha Rao, who has been constantly assisting me in all my book writing endeavours, technical or spiritual.

My sincere thanks to Mrs. M. Prasanna Subha Lakshmi for helping me in all my problems with the computer over the last one year.

I acknowledge the help of my younger brother Dr. Vijaya Gopal for making available several books needed by me.

I thank Mr Nikhil Shah, Proprietor, B.S Publications, for his constant encouragement and assistance.

-Author

Preface

After thirty seven years of active academic service, when I took retirement from Osmania University at Hyderabad in 1997, one year ahead of the scheduled date, my interest in Reiki healings was a turning point in shaping my subsequent life. While I continued to work as Professor and Head of the Electrical and Electronic Engineering Department at Sreenidhi Institute of Science and Technology, Hyderabad, my mind was completely tuned in to find the secret behind healings. I received healing vedic hymns from vedic scholars and practiced them along with Reiki. I became a Reiki master in the year 2000. Mr.William Lee Rand of ICRT, Michigan (U.S.A.) was my master teacher. Healings for different types of problems undertaken by me and my wife proved quite successful even- though some were not. I attended several types of yoga schools. I continued to learn vedic hymns for regular prayer. I received enormous energy and could write three text books for my students of Electrical Engineering in a span of three years. The sales continue to be excellent. I gave several video lessons under SONET project of the government. But, my spiritual thirst prompted me to write a book in Telugu containing the essence of Upanishads. It was titled "Brahmajnana Deepika". It was published by B.S. Publishers.

Over the years I felt that "Sanathana Dharma" or Hinduism was not properly understood by many Hindus themselves. Divine worship became a ritual. Hindus are driven to the point of atheism with no regulatory authority unlike for the others. To be a good citizen one has to be a faithful follower of his own religion. Hinduism, called sanathana dharma, is universal religion. It is the essence of humanism. Vedas are the knowledge revealed to humans by the Divine at appropriate times. They contain everlasting truths. The deep inner meanings of the vedic hymns can be explained only by divine messengers like Shri Adi Shankaraacharya and other great masters.

In this book a sincere attempt is made to bring to the notice of the inquisitive mind an elementary exposure of the vedic literature. Relatively more importance is given to a few topics such as the Vedas, Upanishads, Manusmriti, Yoga science of Patanjali, and Tantra as these have become well known and many would be interested to learn a little more about them. Appropriately the book is titled as "A Vedic Science Primer". Only God has the entire vedic splendor and as such no human can give an insight into it. The vedic splendor creates a magnificent panorama. Only glimpses of it can be provided. The present work may be insignificant but, it is the will of the Divine that it be so.

-Author

Contents

Preamble

If the doors of perception are cleansed, everything would appear to man as it is, infinite.

- William Blake

All religions believe in a supreme being worthy of worship. All religious practices demand a virtuous life. Further, all wrong doings are required to be acknowledged and repented. Justice demands punishment during the life time or after the death for all sins committed. All religions evolved elaborate rituals or practices for worship. Ethical and legal rules are laid out. Philosophical and doctrinal aspects are well established. Architecture and arts are well utilized to present the precepts and perceptions of these religions into the society. In general, ethics and doctrines are created to affirm human values and sustainable social order. Religions are created by men to preserve themselves in a healthy environment. In almost all of these religions Divine inspiration is deeply rooted. Religion offered people a meaning to life beyond the mundane activity. Religion was also a tool to explain transcendental explanation for many of life's mysterious happenings, even if some others feel it is an illusory escapism.

Followers of ancient religions in Mediterranean and the Middle East as well as Norse and Celtic cultures of Northern Europe worshipped several gods. These gods were vested with powers to control moon, stars, mountains and others. Some gods were believed to control such aspects as love, war, strength, and even agriculture and farming.

Egypt: Ancient Egyptians (3100-1000 B.C.) considered their kings (pharaohs) as gods on earth. First they considered Re (also, Ra) as the supreme god. Later, they brought another god, Amon. Subsequently they worshipped a composite god Amon-Re. A great temple was constructed at Luxor for Amon-Re. They believed in an underworld ruled by Osiris and his wife Isis to give judgments to persons after death. The underworld was called Duat. They constructed many temples for several gods. It is noteworthy that importance was given by early Egyptians to moral values and right living and punishments for sinful living. As Ethiopians, Greeks and Persians invaded Egypt, their civilization declined. Upto 6th century C.E. worship of Isis continued.

Greece: Greeks in ancient times (ca. 2500 B.C.) believed that out of Chaos the first god, Gaia was created. Gaia was the earth goddess. She in turn created Uranos, the god of mountains, sky and seas. They together created titans. Titans were giants. Among them Prometheus was important. Zeus was the most important god who along with other 12 gods lived on Mount

Olympus. Poseidon and Hades were the gods that ruled the underworld. Zeus had thunderbolt as his weapon. Other gods and goddesses included Aphrodite, Demeter, Ares, Dionysus and others. After death the souls were to go to Hades across the river Styx, where they undergo punishments for their sinful deeds.

Persia: Persia is modern Iran. Zarathustra founded his religion around 1000 B.C. (There are considerably different opinion about this period. Some put the period around 6000 B.C. while some others place the time around 1200 B.C.).

He is more commonly referred as Zoroaster. According to this religion life is a constant struggle between good gods and evil gods. Zurvan, god of time, who is both male and female, gave birth to Ahura Mazda, the good god and Angra Mainyu, the evil twin. When Ahura Mazda wins the war against his evil twin the whole world would become good.

Mesopotamia: People who inhabited the land between the two rivers, Tigris and Euphrates were called Sumerians, Babylonians, and Assyrians. (ca. 2600-230 B.C.)

They too worshipped several gods created from a primeval sea. These gods later created earth and its inhabitants. They worshipped the sun god Utu , god for life Ninmah and moon god Nanna. Ishtar was the war god. Chaos before creation, was symbolized by goddess Tiamat, the salt water god. Apsu was the fresh water god. Apsu and Tiamat had a son Marderk. Father and son killed Tiamat to create sky and earth with her body.

Rome: Romans adopted the Greek gods. Aphrodite became Venus. Are became Mars. Zeus became Jupiter. Apollo was the god of harmony and civilization. Much of the Greek way of life was adopted by ancient Romans.

Northern Europe: Norway, Sweden, Denmark and Finland are known together known as Nordic region. Ireland, Britain and northern France are included in Celtic region. People who lived in these regions around 1600 - 450 B.C. had their own traditional beliefs. The Norse believed in a tree of life called Yggdrasil. The home of the gods was the top of the tree called Asgard. At the middle of the tree midgard, humans lived. At the roots of the tree underworld exists, and this is ruled by Hel. Here the dead are judged. At the beginning there were ice and fire and when they met, the first to be created was Ymir a giant. A group of gods, Odin, Vili, and Ve together killed Ymir and used his body to create the world. The celts had a sun god called Lugh. Sucellus is the king of all gods. Belanus was the god of healing. Druids were the religious leaders.

Africa: Here people practiced Voodoo. Their deities were Ioa. Rado was the helpful god and Petro the destructive god. In west Africa Vodu was the god. The religion was called Fon. It focused on rituals to summon spirits.

China : Confucianism and Taoism (or Daoism) were the religions that flourished during ancient days in china

Daoism or *Taoism* is attributed to Lao Tzu. There are different speculations about Taoism. It is considered as a successive development by several Taos. Others attribute Taoism to a person Lao Tzu, a contemporary of Confucius. It is believed that both of them actually met once. Lao Tzu was disgusted at the way people lived and left for Tibet. However, at the request of a guard at the border Buddha he wrote his teachings at Hank pass and handed over them to the guard. He composed 500 characters Tao Te Ching meaning 'the way and its powers'. The period was around 531-604 B.C.

It is interesting to note that great masters Plato, Socrates, Buddha, Confucius and Lao Tzu all lived around the same time, the sixth century B.C. According to Daoism Heaven, Water and Earth are considered as gods. Flexibility, Femininity, Humility, Non action and Tranquility are considered virtues. Kong-Fuzi or Kung Fu tzu was the real name of Confucius, (551-479 B.C.) a sage king. Confucius gave moral guidelines for various activities in human life. He taught the importance of family, respect for elders and the need for learning. Five books were said to have been authored by him. They are History, Poetry, Rites, Changes and the Annals of Spring and Autumn. I Ching, the book of changes contains several hexagrams which are used for divination even to day. For the ancient Chinese Di was the ruling god. All natural events were ordained by Di.

The concept of Yin and Yang and Feng Shui are part and parcel of Chinese way of life

While Confucianism stressed on masculine Yang, Daoism emphasized feminine Yin. The ancient culture of China was opposed and systematically eliminated by the communists after 1949.

Japan: . Till Buddhism arrived into Japan from Korea in sixth century of Christian era, Shintoism was the native religion of Japanese. They believed in sacred spirits called Kami. Kami could be anything from mountain, river, person, animal, bird or even an ancestor. The sun goddess was the principal Kami. Gods for happiness and prosperity were called Shichi Fukugin. Inari was worshipped for bestowing food, agricultural prosperity and fertility .

South America : Aztecs and Olmecs (1200 B.C.-300 C.E.) worshipped jaguar as god. It was called Tezcatlipo. Mayan people (300-900 C.E.)

who lived along the west coast of South America built several structures. They evinced interest in astronomy

Modern Religions:

Christianity It is now one of the major religions of the world. Christians believe that God came to earth in the form of Jesus Christ. Christanity developed among ancient Jews. Jesus taught love and nonviolence. 'Love thy neighbor' is an important aspect of this religion. Christians believe that on the seventh day (Sabbath) after creating the world God rested. People should repent for their sins and live correctly. Then eternal life with Him (salvation) is possible. The sermon on the Mount explains the need to love one's enemies. Giving up materialism and obeying God's laws are included in that sermon. Bible and the Church play important role in Christianity.

Islam: Islam is another major religion of the world. Before Islam the Arabs worshipped deities of several gods. Every tribe had its own protecting deity. In Mecca a building called Kaba (cube) contained 360 idols. Mohammed born around 570 A.D. was the prophet who established Islam. The followers of Islam are called Muslims. The basic tenets of Islam include Shahada, Salat, Hajj, Zakat and Sawm. The following constitute the basic tenets of Islam.

There is only one God called Allah.

Pray five times a day facing towards Mecca.

Make a pilgrimage to Mecca at least once in the life time.

Help the needy by giving alms.

Fast during the period of Ramadhan , the ninth month of the lunar year.

Buddhism: Buddhism follows the teachings of Gautam Buddha. Sidhartha born in 480 B.C. at Kapilavastu (present Tilaurkot in Nepal), renounced the worldly life and did penance. After enlightenment he created a monkhood. According to him there are five basic elements in a person namely, physical body, sense perception, ideas, will and consciousness. All these also called skandas, are impermanent and change continuously. Together they make a person. But, there is no self to unite them.

The cycle of birth and death is endless. Nirvana or liberation is possible only with detachment from the world. A favorable birth can be obtained by performing good deeds in this life.

Existence involves suffering

Desire and ignorance are the sources of suffering.

Suffering can be eliminated by destroying desire and ignorance.

Suffering can be eliminated following an eight fold path:

Right understanding, right thought, right speech, right behavior, right occupation, right effort, right contemplation and right concentration. These form the spokes of the wheel of dharma, the righteousness.

Teravada is a branch of Buddhism followed by people living in Sri Lanka, Laos, Thailand, and Cambodia. They follow Buddha's teachings and the scripture 'Tripitaka'. Tripitaka is in Pali language. It contains three parts, discipline, themes and teachings. They do not believe in the theory of Bodhisattvas.

Mahayana branch of Buddhism is followed in China, Tibet, Nepal, Vietnam, Korea and Japan. They believe that enlightenment is open to all (not just limited to monks). They believe in Bodhisattvas, persons who have achieved Nirvana but would like to assist others providing by inspiration so that others too can attain enlightenment. According to Mahayana Bodhisattva possesses generosity, morality, patience, courage, meditation and wisdom as its tenets.

Jainism: Parsvanath (7th or 8th century B.C.) a North Indian prince who renounced the world, preached moral code that included nonviolence, truthfulness, non stealing, and non possession along with sexual renunciation. Mahavira founder of Jainism expanded the teachings of Parsvanath. Much of the suffering in this world is attributed to violence. The senses of the body are to be controlled. Non-violence and vegetarianism are important concepts in this religion. Renunciation of the material world is the means for spiritual advancement.

There is no supreme creator in Jainism. Guidence is taken from a succession of teachers called Jinas. They are also called Titrhankaras. Each Tirthankara is associated with an animal, an object, a pattern or any thing of that type. The last two of them were humans, Parsva and Mahavira. Right knowledge, right conduct, and faith are the corner stones for Jainism. Time is considered infinite and there are cosmic cycles of improvement and decline and at the lowest point of decline a Tirthankara will appear.

Sikhism: Sikhism believes in one God. They had ten gurus or teachers. Nanak (1469-1539) was the first guru who established Sikh religion. Every sikh should observe the five rules –Kesh (uncut hair), Kanga (keep a comb), Kirpan (carry a sword), Kacha (wear short cotton trousers), and Kara (steel or iron bangle). Sikhism believes in moral laws and karma. Actions in this life will influence the life in the next birth. Sikhs try to live well within the family and community. Serving the community and the gurudwara (Sikh place of worship) are ways to liberation. Sikhism emphasizes the need to share wealth with the poor.

CHAPTER 1

Vedas

Vedas: The word veda originated from the root 'vid' meaning 'to know'. Vedas are the off springs of 'vak' or 'shabd' i.e., sound and hence they are eternal. For some Vedas were created by a Divine Being. For some others they had neither a Divine nor a human author, but are eternal. In the beginning of this world all Vedas existed as a single entity. However, in course of time several parts of Vedas were lost. Sage Vyasa (Krishna Dwaipayana) restructured the then existing vedas into four and called them

1. **Rigveda**
2. **Yajurveda**
3. **Samaveda** and
4. **Atharvana veda.**

He allotted these four Vedas to his four disciples – Paila, Vaishampayana, Jaimini and Sumanth for dissemination. As time passed the number of disciples increased and the comprehending power to assimilate vedic knowledge slowly degenerated. This necessitated further division of vedic knowledge. The primary function of Vedas is ritualistic. The vedic texts are recited during ceremonials and are to be understood principally in terms of performance. It is the performance that is important. It gives the writings a meaning.

Whenever vedic hymns are chanted on special occasions the priest who chants Rigvedic mantras or hymns is called *Hotri* and the one who chants Yajurveda is called *Adhvaryu*. The priest who chants Samaveda is called *Udgatri* and the learned one who chants Atharvana veda is called *Brahma*. Brahma is also expected to supervise the entire procedure followed at such rituals and correct if any mistake creeps in knowingly or unknowingly during the performance.

Each veda has basically two identifiable subdivisions, viz. the work part or ritualistic part (*karma kanda*) and knowledge part (*jnana kanda*). The karma kanda has again two distinct parts. The first part, '*Samhita*' deals with mantras (liturgy) or hymns which are metered verses (suktas) devoted to praise of gods invoked during the sacrifices. The other part called '*Brahmanas*' deals with explanations and interpretations for the hymns and contains ritual part of the hymns. Knowledge part or 'jnana kanda' is also subdivided into '*Aranyakas*' and '*Upanishads*'. Aranyakas also called 'forest books' contain matters to be studied in forests, away from the worldly life. The concluding parts of aranyakas are called Upanishads. While several Upanishads are independent some of the Upanishads are mixed with brahmanas and some even form part of Aranyakas. Thus the classification is not rigid. Some scholars classify Aranyakas as belonging to upasana kanda (worship). Upanishads alone are said to belong to jnana kanda. It is the considered opinion of some vedic scholars that only samhitas constitute Vedas and the rest are just adjuncts to Vedas. Vedas are also called 'Srutis' as they were heard from the Divine Spirit by the enlightened rishis or sages. Upanishads were composed probably around 800 B.C.

The sacrifices were later interpreted in terms of development of inner states of beings offering metaphysical explanation regarding the nature of the universe. The comprehension of the ritual is considered more important than the actual performance. For example Brihadaranyakopanishad compares the famous horse sacrifice with the world. The underlying idea of a ritual with respect to the world is explained through Upanishads and hence they give the greatest philosophical exposition of Vedas. Similarly in Brahmanas the power of the ritual is called 'Brahma'. In the context of Upanishads this is understood as the energy underlying both the ritual and the cosmos. This energy is also identified with 'Self' or 'Atma'. This concept is extended to include 'Brahma' as absolute bliss (ananda) and 'chit' or absolute consciousness. Brahma is the absolute essence or absolute 'Truth'.

Rigveda contains prayers to God. These prayers are the greatest truths of existence. Yajurveda describes the ceremonial and ritual aspect of worship. Samaveda contains hymns that praise God and are sung according to metres. Lastly, Atharvana veda contains instructions for maintaining good health and security to the community. The mantra samhitas are metered poems that bestow materialistic prosperity in this world and eternal bliss hereafter. In the following chapters, an account is given about the Samhitas belonging to the four Vedas.

CHAPTER 2

Rigveda (Samhitas)

Rigveda contains 10522 verses included in 1028 suktas (some consider 1017 only, excluding 11 of valakhilyas) which are organized into 10 parts or mandalas. They are all devoted to praise of Gods. 'Rik' means praise. The hymns are composed of meters containing 24 to 104 syllables. The total number of syllables in Rigveda are estimated as 3, 95, 563 organised in 39, 831 padas or words. There is no uniformity since the 'Riks' are the intuitional experiences of various rishis at different points of time from the Divine. These rishis belonged to the same families of - Angirasas, Kanvas, Vasishtas, Vaiswamitras, Atris, Bhrigus, Kashyaps, Agastyas, Bharatas, and others.

The Rigvedic hymns are dedicated to deities such as - Surya., Varuna, Savitur, Indra, Rudra, Ashwins, Maruths, Ushas, Pusha, Brahma, Brihaspathi, Prithvi, Dyaus, Visvedevas and others. Sometimes, different names are used for the same deity.

***Mandala* 1:** It contains 191 hymns and the deity to start with is Agni. He is praised as bestower of wealth. Vayu is invited to drink soma and is praised to give strength along with Varuna and Indra. Aswins are invited to accept sacrificial food. Visvedevas – Indra,Vayu, Brihaspati, Mitra, Agni, Pusha, Bhaga, Adityas, the host of Maruts, Rbhus, Ushas, Heaven, Earth, and even horse, water and grass are invoked to bestow health, wealth and prosperity. This mandala which consists of 2006 verses is composed by several rishis.

***Mandala* 2:** In addition to the deities mentioned in mandala 1, Kapinjala, a bird that brings happy omen and streams of water for bringing prosperity are also praised. There are 43 hymns in this mandala and 429 verses in all. This mandala is mainly attributed to rishi Grtsama Saunahotra.

***Manadala* 3:** It concists of 62 hymns worshipping the same deities as in the previous mandalas. Hymn 3.62.10 has great importance as this is the famous Gayatri mantra which praises Savitur, the Sun god as follows:

"O God thou art the giver of life, the remover of pain and sorrow, the bestower of happiness. O Creator of the universe may we receive Thy Supreme, sin destroying light, may thou guide our intellect in the right direction."

It has 617 verses and rishi Visvamitra Gathinah is credited to be the main composer of this mandala.

***Mandala* 4:** In this mandala, in addition to the usual deities, Dadhikras the horse and Dadhikravan, the stallion and even Ghrita or ghee or clarified butter (the oily substance obtained by boiling butter and used for sacrifice in fire) are praised. There are 58 hymns in this mandala. Vamadeva Gautama is the rishi for this 589 verse mandala.

***Mandala* 5:** It has 87 hymns that praise Agni, Varun, Aswins, Atri, Surya, Savitur, Parjanya, the cloud and Ushas the dawn. Atri clan is mainly responsible for this 727 verse mandala.

***Mandala* 6:** This mandala makes references to Rudra, Mitra Varuna while offering prayers. Interstingly, this mandala has chosen to praise the Cow, Weapons of war and Soma the celebrated drink. In addition Agni, Indra, Visvedevas, Pusha, Aswins, Brihaspati, Heaven and Earth are praised by the rishis. There are 75 hymns in this mandala that include 765 verses attributed to family of Angirasas.

***Mandala* 7:** In this 104 hymn book, for the first time the name of Lord Vishnu appears for worship. Vastospati the protector of homes is also praised. Along with other usual deities the river Sarasvati is mentioned. Frog is praised as it welcomes the first rain. It has 841 verses composed by Vasishta Maitravarun.

***Mandala* 8:** In this 103 hymns book, all the deities that frequently appear in the other mandalas are worshipped and in addition Pavamana and Soma are also worshipped. Several verses of this mandala are due to Kanva clan and some others are due to Angirasas. It also contains 11 hymns that are attributed to Valkhilyas (49-59). In all, this mandala contains 1716 verses.

***Mandala* 9:** This part is completely devoted to Soma Pavamana the purification of Soma drink in 1108 verses composed into 114 hymns. It indicates the importance attached by the early rishis to the Soma drink.

***Mandala* 10:** In this mandala too, the deities Agni, Indra, Varuna, Surya, Soma, Pusha, Brihaspati, Indra, Vaikuntha, Nirrti, Aswins and others are worshipped. In hymn 60 the name Ikshvaku is mentioned. Mention is also made of Yarna, and son of Vaivasvan. It is interesting to note that Faith is praised as follows:

"By Faith Agni is kindled, Through Faith is oblation offered up
We celebrate with praises Faith upon the height of happiness,
Even as the deities maintained Faith in the mighty Asuras
So make this uttered wish of mine true for the liberal worshippers……
Faith in the early morning, Faith at noon day, will we invocate
Faith at the setting of the Sun, O Faith endow us with belief"

(Translation: Ralph T.H. Griffith 1896)

The importance given to faith in Rigveda is highlighted by this translated verse.

There are 191 hymns including 1754 verses. Rivers are praised in Nadi stuti (10.75). The rivers mentioned are counting from west to east – Ganga, Yamuna, Sarasvati, Sutudri (Sutlej), Parusn (Ravi), Asikni (Chenab), Marudvardha,Vipas (Beas), Vitasta (Jhelum), Arjkya, and Susoma. Rivers in present day Afghanistan and Pakistan are also referred. They are Trstama, Susartu, Rasa, Shvetya, Sindhu, Kubha (Kabul), Gomati, Krumu (Khurram), Mehatnu, Silamavati and Urnavati. The last three rivers are not identified as yet.

Hymn 190 explains creation. A verse translated runs as follows:

"From Fervour kindled to its height Eternal Law and Truth were born
Thence was the night produced, and thence the billowy flood of Sea arose, from that same billowy flood of sea the year was after words produced
Ordainer of the days, night, Lord overall who close the eye
Dhatar, the Great Creator, then formed in due order Sun and Moon
He formed in order Heaven and Earth the region of Air and Light."

(Ralph T.H.Griffith)

Mandalas 2 to 7 are the oldest. They are called family books and account for only 38% of the Veda. Mandalas 8 and 9 are of mixed age and account for 15% and 9% of the text. Mandalas 1 and 10 are the later additions accounting for 37% of the books.

It is interesting to note that the number of syllables used in Rigveda are 432000 which is equivalent to the number of muhurtas in 40 years. (One day has 30 muhurtas.)

Originally there were 21 branches or recensions (sakhas) for this veda. But, only six of them are practiced now and the rest are lost. The surviving recensions are Sakala, Bhaskala, Aswalayana, Sankhyayana, Mandukayana, and Aitareya. There are two brahmanas for this veda called Aitareya and Kaushitaki. There are also two aranyakas with the same names. The upanishads associated with this veda are – Aitareya, Kaushitaki, Nadabindu, Atmabodha, Nirvana, Mudgala, Aksharamalika, Tripura, Soubhagya lakshmi and Bahvrycha.

Maha Saura mantrapatha of Rigveda as an example of the type of prayers included in Rigvedic hymns contains several mantras composed in all the seven meters The Sun God is mainly prayed in all these hymns mainly. The great sun god resplendent with all the favorable radiance, rising and ascending the heaven is requested to destroy all maladies, internal and external. He is praised as love incarnate, who does good to all. The one Reality is described in many ways as Indra, the lord of splendour, as Mitra the lord of Ahas, as Varuna, the companion in attendance to Yamini as Agni with ever spreading quality and as Anila (air), the wanderer of skies. The Sun is identified as that one Reality or Supreme Brahma who possesses omnipresence. He who lives in glowing Dyuloka (luminous sky) is the wind in the sky. He is also credited to be the vedic fire in worship and household fire meant for cooking and other purposes. He is in fact the vital energy in humans. He is the regent of the Reality. The sun is prayed to protect from starvation, maladies, bad dreams, and all kinds of evils as he expels darkness and animates the whole world with his radiant rays. The sages prayed Aditya, the sun god, to bestow long life enjoying purity of heart, clear vision, good posterity, free from all ills, ailments and evils so that they can worship Him at every dawn. He is worshipped and prayed to provide happiness to human and cattle and also food, drink, strength and all blessings that are sought.

Rigveda says that after severe penance or tapas, from sankalpa or intention and the 'vak' or word, Brahma (the four faced deity) created day and night. And from them the deep sea and the sky emerged. Later months, seasons, and periods of time came into existence. After creating whole of the universe with time, he pervaded all. He is the Lord, Paramatma. He recreates sun, moon, heaven, earth, the mid region in all ensuing kalpas (periods between evolutions and devolutions) as he did in the past.

CHAPTER 3

Yajurveda (Samhitas)

Yajurveda is completely devoted to formulations for rites and rituals. Yajurveda includes mantras for worshipping God and also vedic rituals related to this worship in addition to the procedures for sacrifices. There are two branches – Krishna Yajurveda and Shukla Yajurveda. Krishna yajurveda contains explanatory portions while Shukla yajurveda consists of mantras only. Originally there were 118 recensions for this veda, 101 for Krishna yajurveda and 17 for Shukla yajurveda. Of these only 51 are practiced now; 32 belonging to Krishna yajurveda and 19 to Shukla yajurveda which incidentally contain some prose passages too.

Basically Yajurveda inspires men to initiate service oriented action. Eventhough it appears as a veda of ritual, in reality it sets forth a yogic practice for purifying and enlightening the body, mind and spirit. This underlying aspect is quite often overlooked.

Shukla yajurveda is practiced in two slightly differing forms called Madhyandina and Kanva variations. Madhyandina is more popular in the northern part of India, while Kanva variation is followed in the south. This veda mainly deals with rituals and sacrifices such as:

New and full moon (Darsa poorna) sacrifices, (chapters 1, 2*)*

Agnihotra (Chapter 3*),*

Somayajna (Chapters 4, 5, 7, 8*)*

Vajapeya, Rajasuya (Chapter 9, 10*) modifications of soma sacrifice*

Agnichayana (Chapters 11, 12, 13, 14, 15, 16, 17, 18*) construction of altars and hearths included.*

Sautramani (Chapters 19, 20, 21*) countering the after effect of excessive soma consumption.*

Aswamedha (Chapters 22, 23, 24, 25*)*

Supplementary rules for various rituals (Chapters 26, 27, 28)

Purushamedha (Chapter 30, 31*)*

Sarvamedha (Chapter 32, 33, 34*)*

Pitruyajna (Chapter 35)
Pravargya (Chapters 36, 37, 38, 39)
Isavasopanishad (Chapter 4)

and others

These are all contained in 40 chapters or adhyayas as indicated.

Yajurveda is the first known book that explained large numbers up to trillion (Parardha). Also, it is the first to explain the concepts of infinity and zero.

Krishna yajurveda contains four popular branches namely, Taittareya, Maitrayani, Charaka-Katha and Kapisthala-Katha samhitas.

Taitariya Samhita contains seven kandas or books subdivided into prapathakas (chapters) and anuvakas (sections).

***Kanda* 1:** It consists of New moon and full moon sacrifices, soma sacrifice, soma cups, rekindling of the fire sacrificial part and rajasuya.

***Kanda* 2:** Special animal sacrifices and the role to be played by hotra at sacrifices are the main items discussed in this kanda.

***Kanda* 3:** It again explains soma sacrifice and some other miscellaneous matters connected with rituals.

***Kanda* 4:** Preparation of fire place or hearth, laying of the bricks, offering to Rudra and preparation of fire are topics discussed in this kanda.

***Kanda* 5:** This kanda explains the procedure for placing fire in the fire pan, fire altar and its features and horse sacrifice.

***Kanda* 6:** It contains exposition of soma sacrifice as well as Dakshna to be given to the priests. Further this kanda explains Agnistoma, Atiratra, Dwiratra, Pancharatra, Angirases and other rituals. Aswamedha or horse sacrifice is further considered in this kanda.

***Kanda* 7:** In this last book soma sacrifice is further explained highlighting its importance.

Each of these samhitas have Brahmanas associated with them. Some of them have aranyakas and upanishads associated with them. The list is vast and is not given here. Sathapatha brahmana is the famous brahmana that belongs to Shukla yajurveda.

There are 1975 hymns in this veda and each hymn must accompany an act of sacrifice. For example Taittareya aranyaka explains five sacrifices that are ought to be performed by every householder. They are:

Deva yajna – offering to devas or gods

Pitruyajna – offering libations to pitrus or ancestors,

Bhuta yajna – offering bali or foodstuff to all creatures,

Manushya yajna – offering food to guests, and

Brahma yajna – chanting Vedas (praying the God)

This daily routine constitutes an important tradition

Vedas specify Srauta yajnas of three kinds.

Paka yajna which is to be performed on the first day of lunar fortnight at home and involves in offering sthalipakam (food cooked at home) to sacrificial fire.

Havir yajna: This is performed at a general sacrificial place called 'yagasala'. This ritual is performed as 'darsa' or the day of first sighting of moon and 'poorna' on the day following full moon.

Soma yajna: This consists of elaborate rituals for sacrifice (stoma). For this yajna hotr, adhvaryu, udgatri and brahma must be present, each along with three more priests to assist them making the total number of priests to 16. Further, there are seven types of somayajnas detailed in Vedas. They are – agnistoma, atyagnistoma, uktya, sodasi, vajapeya, atiratra and aptoryama.

The famous Rudram and Chamakam mantras used in worshipping Lord Shiva while bathing the Shiva in the 'Linga' form are from this veda (4.7 to 4.9). Also the Maha Mrutyunjaya mantra is also from this veda (1.8.6):

"Tryakbakam Yajamahe Sugandhim Pushtivardhanam
Urvaruka miva Bandhanan Mrityormukshiyamritat"

It has the following meaning

"To Tryambaka we make offering The Fragrant, Increaser of prosperity
Like a cucumber from its stem. From death may I be loosened not from immortality."

(Arthur B. Keith -1914)

Information contained in some of the verses is briefly presented:

- The Supreme Lord is prayed to inspire humans to perform good deeds.
- Accept the Truth and sacrifice life to protect the Truth.
- Perform assigned duties without fear.
- Knowledge is radiant.
- Knowledge should lead one to tread the path of Truth. Agni is worshipped to protect the body, to bestow long life and bless with radiance.
- Work minded people speak softly.

- Sun god is prayed for giving protection.
- Agni is worshipped to liberate from wrong doings and to inspire to do good deeds.
- For steadiness of mind Agni is prayed to.
- Wise men following the path of truth should not be short tempered, proud and aggressive.
- Married couple should engage in good deeds. Women should not fear their husbands.
- Yama and niyama (physical and mental discipline) are to be followed. God is to be worshipped to remove defects and demerits and be bless with steady mind, health and energy.
- Happiness can be achieved only by working constantly according to abilities and limitations.
- Taking medicines is advised for maintaining health when required.
- With the grace of Lord Rudra the entire universe can be devoid of ailments and live with constructive thinking.

  (This is in conformity with the adage that a healthy mind lives in healthy body and is from the famous Rudra mantra :

  " Yathanaha Sarvamijjagada Yakshmam Sumana Asat"
- Good thoughts purify the mind.
- From Namakam we have mantras such as

" Vajachchame Prasavasche me Prayatischche me Prasitischcha me
Dhitischche me Kratuschcha me Swarachche me Shlokaschcha me
Shravashcha me Shrutishcha me Jyotischcha me Swshcha me.... Yajnena Kalpantam"

This is an invocation to the Lord Rudra to bless with food, comforts, perseverance, mental power, soft and good speaking power, strength for doing good deeds, sacrifices, and for praying the Lord as well as for power to listen. There are many more such prayers.

- The source of knowledge is within.
- Self restraint is essential for happy life.
- With determination intelligence, with intelligence devotion and with devotion truth can be reached.
- By Realizing the ultimate truth, that is attaining true knowledge, one can get all the comforts needed such as food, power, glory and other things.

- Goddess Saraswati symbolizing knowledge, is worshipped and prayed for enlightening the mind with knowledge in the same way as she illumines the vast expanse of sky.
- The Gayatri mantra appears as:

" Aum Bhur Bhuva Swaha

Tat Savitor Varenyam

Bhargo Devasya Dhimahi

Dhiyo Yo Nah Prachodayaat"

"Aum, the Pranava the Supreme Cosmic Soul is the Creator of this universe. He is the one who nurtures and enlightens all the creation. He is chaste and worthy of worshipping. Placing that Savitur with great devotion in the heart leads to good thoughts and good actions. Peace, happiness and prosperity will result".

The importance of yajna is highlighted. It is the medium through which one can obtain vital energy, good sight and hearing capacity, excellent communication skills. Yajna elevates one spiritually kindling the flame of knowledge within. But one should perform yajna for its own sake.

Exerting absolute control on mind is essential.

- God is to be prayed to destroy evil and bring good to all. The spiritually elevated should practice penance.
- Taking the advice of learned experts is suggested for all purposes.
- The one who understands that the Supreme Soul is like the Sun beyond the darkness, will be liberated from death and there is no other way than this.

" Rucham Brahmam Janayanto Deva Agre Tada Bruvan

Yasvaivam Brahmano Vidyat. Tasya Deva Asan Vashe."

"Those who have realized the Supreme Nature of the lord will be able to control everything. Senses do not motivate but will work as desired". This is from Purusha suklam.

From Maha Sauram we have

"Udutyam Jatavaedasam Devam Vahanti Ketavaha

Drishe Viswaya Suryam."

Learned persons should share their knowledge about the Absolute Reality with others in the same way as the Sun distributes his effulgence.

Yajurveda is considered as representative of the totality of transforming, processing and interpreting apparatus of Riks.

CHAPTER 4

Samaveda (Samhitas)

Samaveda is also the word of God revealed in the beginning of creation for the moral, spiritual, economic and physical guidance and upliftment of humanity. This veda is to be chanted or sung at certain sacrifices and rituals. It is said that only 75 of the hymns are of its own while the rest are taken from Rigveda. According to Devichand – "a verse can have different meanings according to its different devatas (subject matters). The identity of a verse at different places does not connote repetition". Samaveda deals with upasana or worship and contemplation. There are in all 1875 verses or hymns in Samaveda. The Gods praised in this veda are Agni, Indra and Soma.

There are three parts in this veda – Purvarchika, Uttararchika and Maha Namni archika

There are further subdivisions which are not necessary at this level of introduction.

According to Vishnu purana Sama veda has 1000 sakhas or recensions. Of these only three are surviving now. They are Kauthuma (Gujarat) Ranayaniya (Maharastra) and Jaiminiya (Karnataka). This veda is sung by Udgatri during special occasions as per specific meters or chandas. These meters are – Gayatri, Ushnik, Anushtup, Brihati, Pankti, Trishtup, and Jagati which correspond to the seven colours of the spectrum of white light, namely, red, orange, yellow, green blue, indigo, and violet. According to Prof Tony Nader Ram Samaveda is the sum total of all that is pertaining to Samhitas from a very keen observation point of the concerned Rishis. This Veda, thus represents "the totality of sensory systems, and perceptual apparatus including receptor, channels, pathways, and structures involved in organizing, maintaining balance, and identifying and decoding inputs and information. The wakeful physiology receives all the flow of experience through these channels. They sustain the quality of flowing wakefulness". This is the observation of Prof Tony Nader Ram.

For the purpose singing Samaveda hymns they are further altered by prolongation, repetition and insertion of stray syllables and other modifications. In this Veda a systematic procedure is adopted that gives melody, to a chanted verse. All verses in the same chapter or Adhyaya have the same meter and one deity (Adhidevata).

Each Sama Veda mantra is marked with one or two of seven signs - 1, 2, 3 and consonants u, ra, ka and absence of any sign. This is the basic Sama Veda. The basic Sama is expanded in the second stage by adding new vowels modifying some syllables and adding numerals at various points to denote the time duration of singing these syllables. From 1875 verses 2722 ganas are thus obtained. These ganas are sub divided into four types. They are Gramageya or general type (1197), Aranyageya, for forest singing (294), Uha or extrapolations (1026) and Uhya or level (205).

To sing Samas correctly the rishis developed a technique similar to modern parity control in computer engineering. This is contained in Samaveda Samhita by Pandit Sripad Damodar Satvalekar (1956; 4th edition)

Purvarchika: There are 640 verses contained in the four Kandas of Purvarchika, Agneya kanda, Ayendra kanda, Pavamanam kanda and Aranyak kanda divided further into 6 books. A book is a prapathaka and a chapter is an ardh prapathaka. The important items in the various books and chapters are summarized:

Book 1

Chapter **1:** God the giver of pleasures and the fruits of actions is praised in this part.

Chapter **2:** God the giver of cattle, wealth, speech, is prayed to give knowledge. Here, thirty three gods consisting of 12 Adityas, 11 Rudras, 8 Vasus, Indra and Prajapati are mentioned as the companions of the Supreme Lord.

Book 2

Chapter **1:** God created this world with 7 mothers (earth, water, fire, air, ether, intellect and ego). Singing praise of God is advocated. Knowledge can be acquired through yoga and breath control with His grace.

Chapter **2:** Soul that enters the womb of a woman is enlightened by the food she takes.

Book 3

Chapter **1:** It includes praising of God for prosperity, wealth, guidance, fulfillment of wants. Soul is hailed.

Chapter **2:** The oneness of the God and soul is brought out. The importance of time or 'kaala' is stressed by mentioning that the Cosmic mind moves in thirty steps. It means that there are 30 muhurtas (each of 48 minute duration) in a day of 24 hours.

Book 4

***Chapter* 1:** Knowledge is acquired through yoga. Deep breath prolongs life. Knowledge is the birth right of the soul. Chanting of Vedas loudly leads to acquisition of knowledge. Some times soul is equated to God in this chapter.

***Chapter* 2:** Enlightement of soul can be achieved through yoga. Prana and Apana, the vital airs are praised as the companions of the soul.

Book 5

***Chapter* 1:** It explains that God is leaderless, companionless and unrivalled. Yoga and penance leads to all joys.

***Chapter* 2:** Charity leads to peace, knowledge and wealth. Knowledge, action and contemplation as 'Jnan', 'Karma' and 'Upasana' are the basic things that each of the four Vedas contain. A yogi realizes the lofty Light of the Divine in his own Soul.

Book 6

***Chapter* 1:** As Sun drives away darkness, so also the Soul should get rid of all the sins and shortcomings. Vedas are revealed at the beginning of every cycle of creation in the hearts of sages. God, yogi and soul are praised. The ten vital airs are mentioned.

***Chapter* 2:** Even Soul cannot transgress Vedas. Yogi and soul are mentioned as great like god and are extolled. Devotion to the Creator is to be propagated among people.

***Chapter* 3:** This chapter is called Aranyak kanda and some consider it as separate from Purvarchika.

OM is considered as the best of all the words in Vedas. Acquisition of wealth should not be for selfish needs but should be for community welfare. The eternal nature of the Soul is described. The Supreme Lord with one fourth of His Grandeur created this universe and with three fourth of his Grandeur rose higher than all, separate from the universe, and there remained in a blissful state. Earth revolves in space along with its mother, water. Prayers and praises revolve around God, Sun and Soul.

In Maha-namn-yarchika God is prayed for knowledge, celibacy, spiritual knowledge, prosperity, protection and nourishment.

Uttararchika:

Book 1

Contains Paryers to God as usual. The path of Yoga is pursued for knowledge. Prana and Apana are said to be the masters of strength. Fair distribution of food to all people is requested. Protection is requested for

100 years. Brihat Sama has to be chanted for safety of Yajna. Medicinal herbs must get good exposure to sun for effective working. Soma, Yogi and Soul are exalted. Soma, when given as oblation to fire rises to sky and comes back as rain. Dakshina or gifts as gold and money must be given to priests without their asking for it.

Book 2

Soul is strengthened by observance of yama and niyama rules connected with the disciplining of body and mind. Udgathas are urged to sing Brihatsama. The voice of the inner soul can be heard in the heart. Soma thrills through 21 channels composed of, mind, ten vital airs and ten organs of cognition and works. Soul also moves through the five koshas or sheaths – physical, vital, mental, knowledge and bliss. God never fails his worshippers. Soul through intellect, ego and mind retains truth and wisdom of God.

Book 3

He residing in all the bodies, is found seated in the soul. Lust or anger degrades the soul. The virtues of prana, apana and soma are highlighted. Soma is praised as sharpener of intellect. The lovely soul manifests itself in the heart. Yajnas purify earth and heaven. Hearing Vedas gives intelligence. Soul manifests itself as the creator of all the mental feelings including touch, vision, sight, speech, and hearing. Vedas and Upavedas the eight footed knowledge is supported by nine parts, namely, the six Vedangas, Nighantu or the vedic word glossary, Dharmasastra or the code of moral conduct and Mimamsa or correct interpretation of vedic rituals, dispelling doubts of all sorts. Knowledge and action take the Soul to God like horses.

Book 4

Yoga, yogi, soul and soma are exalted in this part. God is enthusiastically praised. God is also identified with guru or teacher. While God pervades the universe soul pervades the body. Soul should be purified with noble ideas and spiritual knowledge. The duties of the soul are spreading of happiness and curbing of evil thoughts. The speciality of Sushumna nadi or nerve channel that lies in the middle of the spinal column is mentioned. This is the channel through which the mystic Kundalini power flows. An eloquent appeal is made to all, to sing the glory of God. The true knowledge of God is spread in all religions.

Book 5

Yogi purifies his body and mind with yama and niyama regulations which are ten in number. Seven thoughts meaning concentration on the seven yogic centres 'chakras' (plexuses) in and above the body will lead to great joy. God is prayed to rain happiness on Earth. This indicates the universal nature of vedic religion. Intellectuals, the wise and the learned are praised highly. Knowledge, meditation and action are the three voices of the worshipper. Celibacy leads to body lustre and strong mind. The Omnipresent, The Omnipotent and The Omniscient God is praised lavishly for all the Grace that He bestows on His creation.

Book 6

Life is, Yajna, a sacrifice. The world is enjoyed by learned persons with the power of knowledge and meditation. Ordinary mortals can not understand God's revelation. Only a yogi can comprehend. The higher goal has to be visualized in the soul. God is to be prayed to bless with plenty of rain so that food is made available. Vedic verses are all revealed in seven sister meters, namely Gayatri, Anushtup, Trishtup, Ushnik, Jagati, Pankti, and Brihati. In this book considerable emphasis is laid on yoga, deep meditation or 'Samadhi' and acquiring knowledge through yoga. It is reemphasized that Self realization and thereby realization of God is possible for a yogi.

Book 7

Supreme happiness is felt by the dynamic soul through the nourishing rays of knowledge. God is the revealer of all the vedic verses. He is requested to protect humanity with the three Vedas. Soul is invincible. In the yajna of life soul goes ahead of mortal men. It is a fast and convenient vehicle for the journey of life. Fire (Agni) is prayed to give happiness. Again, God and soul as Indra and Agni are invoked for spiritual power and are requested to destroy passions and provide divine knowledge. Through regular breathing process the soul is said to perform yoga yajna. The teacher and the disciple are advised to imbibe the truth. The Vedas are the authority for excellence.

Book 8

Worshipping several gods like Indra, Varuna and others is in fact worshipping the one and the only one God. Agni or fire is prayed to give protection and riches. Self realization is likened to drinking a juice happily. Yajna brings rain to earth and nourishes it. Body is the chariot and mind is the guide. Soul residing in the body acquires knowledge and performs noble deeds with the help of the ten organs. Control these ten organs with the ten vital airs (prana, apana, vyana, udana, samana, naga, kurma, krikra, devadatta and dhananjaya). God created this universe and pervaded it through out. Reference is made to soma drink in this book. Indra-Agni or God and Soul or Sun and Lightning are praised. Yogis can comprehend the Vedas. Prana and apana are extolled for their capacity to bring happiness. Morning, noon and evening prayers are to be performed. Prana and apana are called Aswins the twin deities. Prana, apana and Om are together considered as a three wheeled chariot and worshipping them brings universal prosperity.

Book 9

Soul is to be purified by the seven forces (two eyes, two ears, two nostrils and mouth). Yajna causes rain. Om when chanted will lead to realizing the divinity. One who dies takes birth again in another body. Mitra, Aryaman and Varuna are to realized in the three arteries of the spinal cord Ida, Pingala and Sushumna through yoga. Knowledge gives joy to the world as mothers nourish their children. God, the Lord of all is requested to give safety and prosperity.

Like other Vedas, Sama veda also is mainly concerned with prayers to the One God known by different names to give material and spiritual prosperity. The majority of the verses praise the glory of the Lord. They also exalt the learned, yogis and sages who have attained high level of spiritual knowledge.

CHAPTER 5

Atharvanaveda (Samhitas)

Atharvanaveda: The first son of Hiranyagarbha was Atharva or Atharvan. Hence, this Veda is known as Atharva veda or Atharvana Veda. According to tradition this book was composed mainly due to the effort Bhrigus and Angirasas. Other rishi families such as Kaushiks, Vasishtas, Kashyaps are also connected with the composition of this veda. There were originally 9 recensions or schools of this veda. They are:

Paippalada
Stauda
Mauda
Saunakiya
Jajala
Brahmadarsa
Devadarsa
Charana vidya

Of these only two recensions – Saunakiya and Paippalada survived. This veda is concerned with curing of diseases, acquiring wealth, and matters related to mundane life. It contains knowledge pertaining to materialistic prosperity. It consists of about 6000 verses constituting the 731 hymns, grouped into 20 books. This veda also deals with knowledge about warfare, military practices and related subjects.

There is evidence which shows that at the time when Atharvanaveda was composed Pleides occupied spring equinox. The latest date of this occurrence was about 2200 B.C. Hence, one may consider the possibility of all other vedas being revealed much before that date. This is evident from Atharvanaveda itself which says:

"In whom exists the first born sages

And Rik, Saman and Yajus and the earth..."

It is clear that the three Vedas existed even before the earth was created and later Atharvanaveda came into existence. Some points in the twenty books of this veda are presented briefly.

Book 1

It contains prayers to Vachaspati, Varun, Indra, Agni, Brihaspsti, Soma and other gods for protection, health, long life and prosperity. It contains mantra charms for protection against evil spirits, fever, diseases like dysentery, constipation, headache, cough. Mantras for punishment of enemies are also given. The special features are a benediction on a king at consecration ceremony as well as an invocation for invisibility. It has 35 hymns in all.

Book 2

In addition to the prayers to gods like Agni, Indra, and others there are invocations for a child's long life, absolution and benediction on homeward coming cattle. Charms to work against fever, enemies, friends, magic and all sorts of worms are given. A charm for getting a suitable husband for a bride is also included. There are 36 hymns in this kanda.

Book 3

A song of harvest, prayer for love and concord in family, a farmers' prayer, a benediction on a newly constructed house, taming and training of an elephant, removal of women's sterility and invocation for male progeny are special features in this book: Charms for personal benefits, recovery of sick persons, against rheumatism and for prosperity are also mentioned. Agni is prayed as in other books. It contains 31 hymns.

Book 4

Agni, Indra, Maruts, Heaven and Earth, Bhava, Sarva, Mitra-Varuna, Manyu and other deities are prayed for bestowing health and prosperity. Charms for super human sight (divya drshti), and for accelerating the onset of rains are incorporated in this book. There are also benedictions to newly crowned king, cows and milk caldron. In all this book consists of 40 hymns.

Book 5

There are prayers to presiding deities of directions (dikpalakas) in addition to the gods in the previous books. Charms for general prosperity, and for increase in cattle strength, for destruction of malignant goblins and against diseases are given. It has 31 hymns in all.

Book 6

Prayers to Savitur, Indrà, Agni, Brihaspati, Soma, Maruts, Waters, Rivers, Surya the Sun God and Vaisvanara are contained in this book. Invocations for protection, long life, peace, security, strength, mental preservation, forgiveness of sins, are included in this book. Charms for love, power, preeminence and similar other mundane desires are provided in this kanda.

An invocation to promote growth of hair, a thanks giving prayer, charms connected with love affairs, and benediction on a new born are special features in this book of 142 hymns.

Book 7

Praise of Agni, Atharvan, Sun, Vayu, Aditi, Adityas, Saraswati, Savitur, Yama, Vishnu, Varuna, Brihaspati, Vak, Aswins, new moon, full moon, Rudra as Agni and further prayers for protection, timely rains, good health, wealth, children and for deliverance from sins are contained in this book. Charms against trouble, evils and diseases are presented. Victory in battles and success in love matters are other topics dealt in this book of 118 hymns.

Book 8

Glorification of Viraj, charms for destruction of hostile army, and demons and restoration of health to sick person are high lights of this book of 10 hymns.

Book 9

Evolution of Viraj, nature and Maya are the cosmogonical topics explained in this book. Chandasas Gayatri, Anushtup, Trishtup, Jagati, and Brihadarki are mentioned. It explains that there is an order in the evolution of the universe. The last and tenth hymn speaks about – "they call the cold months six and six the hot ones" may indicate the early existence of Aryans at the north pole where there are only two seasons. This kanda has 10 hymns.

Book 9

Glorification of kama, the desire and charms for various diseases are found in this book. The four stages of vak or speech are implicitly told. The one God is explained to be known with several names. This book has 10 hymns.

Book 10

In this book of 10 hymns Skambha an infinite pillar that was Brahma the Supreme Reality is discussed. All the gods worship this Skambha. The creation of Purusha and passing of Brahma into that Purusha, the golden castle with great brilliancy is mentioned.

Book 11

Prayers to deities, incantations for destroying enemies and glorification of sacrificial substances are the topics of this book. Agni is praised for giving benefits to learners of Vedas. It highlights the fact that "Gods made the mortal their abode and entered and possessed the man". There are 10 hymns in this part.

Book 12

In all there are only 5 hymns in this book containing mainly, prayers to Earth or Prithvi and procedures for sacrificial offerings to gods by householder and his wife for prosperity in life in this world and in the other world (heaven).

Book 13

This book contains 4 hymns dedicated mainly to the glorification of Rohita (fire) and the Sun God.

Book 14

It contains only two hymns describing the marriage ceremonies concerning bride of Surya. It contains the epigram that "Truth is the base that bears the Earth"

Book 15

All the 18 hymns of this book are about 'Vratya' the wandering monk. Prajapati the Patriarch created Mahadeva who expanded himself in all the four directions. He is identified as time or 'Kaala', and is said to have stood on four legs or the four seasons that later became six (seasons or Ritus, each of two months). He is seas, rains and everything. He is also Satva, Rajas and Tamas, the three states of balance, action and inaction of existence.

Book 16

There are 9 hymns in this book. Preparation of holy water to purify and give freedom from sin, charms to secure power, long life, blessings and avert evil dreams and an imprecation on enemy are main contents of this book.

Book 17

This single hymn book is dedicated to the worship of Indra identified with both Vishnu and Sun.

Book 18

The four hymns of this book deal with verses connected with funeral rituals.

Book 19

Benedictory hymns to Brahma, to night, to Kama or desires, to time or kaala, to sleep, for love, long life and prosperity are given in this book. Prayers to Agni, Waters, Sun, Ushas or dawn, and rishis of Adharvana Veda are the other features of this book. Charms for prosperity and against evils are given as in other books. The chief vedic meters Gayatri, Ushnik,

Anushtup, Brihati, Trishtup, and Jagati are mentioned. The famous Purusha suktha is the highlight of this 71 hymn book.

Book 20

There are 143 hymns in this last book of the Veda. Prayers to gods, Charms for various benefits and against evil forces as well as imprecations are present which need no special mention.

There is considerable symbolism in Atharvana Veda hymns. These verses with their meanings can be broadly classified as under :

- Prayers to Devas.
- Health, healing and physiology.
- Stages of life learning phase (brhmacharya), living phase (householders' duty) and ascetic phase.
- Governance, nation, community welfare and cosmopolitan outlook.
- Spiritual and psychological topics.
- Creation, the creator and cosmogony.
- Ayurvedic concepts: General treatment, cures, germ eradication, antidotes to poison, germ therapy, Charms or Kavachas for protection.
- Arrow and reed are used symbolically for health and bliss.
- Marriage: Happy life of man and woman through the institution of marriage is prescribed.
- Castes: Only three castes are mentioned – Priests or Brahmins, Royalty or Kshatriyas and Workers or Vishas. All traders and workers are grouped as one.
- Universal brotherhood: Gods are prayed to

"Create between us and strangers a unity of hearts". and

" may we not fight against the divine spirit within us..." This is the spirit of vedic culture itself.

Atharvana Veda supports the union of hearts and minds and freedom from hatred. The existence of several religious practices and several languages in different lands are recognized and respected.

There are several good sayings in Atharvana Veda such as :

- Sun is the soul of all that is dynamic and static.
- Life has to be faced with heroic attitude.
- Let everyone be happy and be peaceful.

Agni is identified on several occasions as will power and is prayed to destroy the six internal enemies.

Atharvana veda represents the muscular and skeletal system in human body (Veda Purusha) as this system contains the organs of action.

It is believed that when God manifested himself at the time of creation as Pranavanaada AUM, Brahma prayed for knowledge and God ideated Vedas from Pranava,- Rigveda out of A, Yajurveda from U, Samaveda from M and Atharvanaveda from the arthmatra.

Esoterically, pure light with its motion created Vak (word) which with further mutation with Prana (breath) became successively Para, Pashyanti, Madhyama and Vaikhari vak. The spoken word is vaikhari. It has its roots in madhyama. The cause of madhyama is pasyanti. The origin of pasyanti is para vak. Para is the chaitanya from which speech springs.

Vedic hymns are chanted in five different ways. They are – mula, pada, krama, jata and Ghana.

In mula hymns are chanted continuously.

In pada they are split word by word.

In krama the padas are joined as 1, 2 -2, 3 – 3, 4 - and so on.

In jata padas are joined, recited in textual order and then in reverse order and then again in textual order as 1,2 – 2,1 – 1,2 – 2,3 – 3,2 -2,3 – and so on.

Finally, in Ghana complicated combinations such as 1, 2 – 2,1 – 1, 2, 3, - 3, 2, 1 -1, 2, 3 etc., are used.

CHAPTER 6

Brahmanas

Brahmanas are ritualistic specific like Yajurveda, but are later additions and not as old and esoteric enough as the Vedas. The rituals are meant to portray in real life, a cosmic ritual symbolically. External rituals are symbolic of internal processes. The power of the ritual lies in the mantra chanted. The metric mantra chanting attunes the person to the cosmic vibrations and puts in tune with the transformative force of nature. This enables one to perform right action. The sacrifice is the sacred nature and movement of life. For example Aitareya Brahmana contains Soma sacrifices. Panchavimsa Brahmana specifies the duties of Udgars. Vamsa Brahmana gives succession of teachers and disciples. Sevaral rituals are synchronized to seasons and equinoxes and thus form the basis to calendar.

Rigvedic Brahmanas

1. Shakala Sakha: Aitareya Brahmana or Aswalayana Brahmana.
2. Bhaskala sakha: Koushitaki Brahmana or Sankhyayana Brahmana.

Yajurveda Brahmanas: For both the recessions there are Brahmanas.

Krishna Yajurveda Brahmanas are integrated into samhitas. These are:

Maitrayini samhita

Charaka or Katha samhita

Kapisthala Katha samhita and Taittariya samhita

Taittariya Brahmana is also existing.

Shukla Yajurveda: There are again two saakhas.

Vajasaneyi Madhyandina - Satapatha Brahmana

Kanva – Satapatha Brahmana.

Samaveda Brahmanas: Kauthuma – Panchavimsa Brahmana
Shadvimsa Brahmana
Samavidhana Brahmana
Arseya Brahmana
Devatadhyana Brahmana

Chandogya Brahmana or Mantra Brahmana

Vamsa Brahmana

Jaiminiya Brahmana

Jaiminiya Arseya Brahmana

Jaiminiya Upanishad Bahmana.

Atharvana Veda Brahmanas: Gopatha Brahmana

To make the importance of brahmanas clear Sathapatha brahmana (madhyandina) is chosen for a little elaboration.

Sathapatha brahmana: This Brahmana with 14 Kandas or parts divided into about 100 adhyayas (one hundred paths) contains about 360 brahmanas. This famous brahmana contains myths of creation, the story of Manu and the great deluge, elaborate description of preparation of altars, ceremonial objects, recitations during the rituals, soma libation and others. Several adhyayas are close commentaries for Yajurveda samhitas. For example detailed procedures connected with Agnyavadhana, Agnihotra, Pindapitruyajna, Agrayaneshti, Chaturmasyani, Agnishtoma, Agnichayana, Aswamedha, Pravargya Darsapoorna, Vajapeya, Rajasuya and other rituals and sacrifices are discussed in greater detail.

There are implicit in these rituals certain cosmogonic hidden meanings. For example the bricks used in the contruction of an altar or fire place are said to represent days and nights. The whole altar then represents the year. Year is the prajapathi (patriarch).

The killing of Vritra by Indra is an interesting story. Vritra is covering of space. Indra destroyed it with Vajra or thunder bolt. It may be conjectured that through an electrifying process applied to the plasma in space, creation started.

CHAPTER 7

Aranyakas

Aranyakas deal with the mystic teachings of the sacrificial religion. Aranyakas also contain ritual passages but with philosophical texts. These Aranyakas are supposed to have been developed some time from 900 to 600 B.C. The widely known Aranyakas are Aitareya, Taittariya, Sankhayana and Brihadaranyaka. Aranyakas mean forest or wilderness books.

Aitareya Aranyaka: There are 5 chapters in this. Chapter 1 describes Mahaa vrata a regimen. Chapters 4, 5 and 6 of this Aranyaka constitute Aitareyopanishad. Chapter 3 elaborates pada patha, krama-patha and the like and is a samhitopanishad explaining about Veda recitation and swaras. The mantras of chapters 4 and 5 belong to "mahanaamni" meant for the ritual "Madyandina". Chapter 2 explains "Prana vidya". It is interesting to find a comparision between some sages and prana. Prana is Viswamitra as viswa means the universe and mitra is the sustainer. Prana is also Vaama Deva as vaama means respectful and worshipful. It is also Atri since "traayate" signifies prana that protects. Again, "bhaara" is supporting and "vaaja" means mortal body and prana entering the body makes it mobile, so that Bharadwaja means prana. Finally, prana is Vasishta since "vas" means living in the body of senses. Following vedic procedures one may attain a higher birth (even divine) and disobeying them may lead to lower births subsequently.

Taittariya Aranyaka: There are 10 chapters in this Aranyaka.

Chapter 1: It contains the famous "Suryanamaskaras" or prostrations to the Sun God with Chants.

Chapter 2: This explains the five sacrificial rituals or yajnas a Brahmin has to perform daily to propitiate his sins. The sacredness of 'Yajnopavita' (the sacred thread), Sandhya worship, worshipping of the manes, Brahma yajna, 'kushmanda homa' a home cleansing sacrifice are contained in this chapter.

Chapters 3 and 4 also explain certain other sacrificial offerings and the technicalities involved there in.

Chapter 5: is a treatise on Yajnas or sacrifices.

Chapter 6 deals with "pitru medha" rituals connected with disposal of dead body.

Chapters 7, 8 and 9 constitute Taittariya Upanishad which is considered later.

Cahpter 10 a very long one contains Maha Narayanopanishad.

Sankhayana Aranyaka: This Aranyaka contains 15 chapters.

Chapters 1 and 2 deal with "maha vrata" a ceremony.

Chapters 3 to 6 costitute Kaushitaki Upanishad.

Chapters 7 and 8 constitute Samhitopanishad.

Chapter 9 explains the greatness of Prana, the life sustaining force.

Chapter 10 explains the esoteric implications of 'Agnihotra' the sacrificial fire. Purusha, the human and the Divine is a synthesis of Agni the fire as speech (Vak), air as prana, sun as eyes, moon working through the mind, directions (dik) through ears and water in the potency. If this truth is understood then one can comprehend that all sacrifices offered into fire reach the god in heaven.

Chapter 11 contains a verse that is antidote to death and sickness.

Chapter 12 explains the fruits of worship.

Chapter 13 emphasizes the need for detachment and the path of "sravana, manana and nidhi dhyasana" (hearing, repeating and contemplating) for enlightenment is explained. The practice of penance, faith and other qualities for spiritual elevation are mentioned.

Chapter 14: It has only two verses. It contains the most important statement "I am Brahma". Again chanting a mantra without knowing its meaning is like an animal carrying load without knowing what it contains.

Chapter 15 includes the genealogy of spiritual teachers from Brahma to Sankhayana.

It is the considered opinion of an acknowledged scholar that Aranyakas are the Brahmanas of Secrets.

CHAPTER 8

Upanishads

Upanishads: There are in vogue now only 108 upanishads as mentioned in Muktikopanishad eventhough originally there were 1180. They are given as follows:

Upanishads associated with Rigveda are 10, while originally they were 21.

Upanishads associated with Yajurveda are 51, while originally they were 109:

With Shukla Yajurveda they are19 and

With Krisna Yajurveda they are 32 now existing.

Upanishads associated with Samaveda are 16 while originally they were 1000 and

Upanishads associated with Atharvanaveda are 31 existing now out of 50 that prevailed once. Thus, while the original branches were 1180, now only 108 are practiced. These are:

Those belonging to Rigveda – Aitareya, Kaushitaki, Nada bindu, Atma Bodha, Nirvana, Mudgala, Akshara Malika, Tripura, Sowbhagya Lakshmi and Bahrvyucha;

those belonging to Shukla or white Yajurveda – Eesavasya, Brihadaranyaka, Jabala, Hamsa, Paramahamsa, Subala, Mantrika, Niralamba, Trisikhi brahmana, Mandala brahmana, Advayataraka, Paigala, Bhikshuka, Turiyavatitavadhuta, Adhyatma, Tarasara, Yajnavalkya, Sathyayaneeya, and Muktika;

those belonging to Krishna or black Yajurveda – Katha, Taittreya, Brahma, Kaivalya, Swetasvatara, Garbha, Narayana, Amritabindu, Amritanada, Kalagni Rudra, Kshurika, Sarvasara, Sukarahasya, Tejobindu, Dhyanabindu, Brahmavidya, Yogatattva, Dakshinamurthi, Skanda, Sareeraka, Yogasikha, Ekakshara, Akshi, Avadhuta, Katha Rudra, Rudrahrydaya, Yogakunda, Pancha Brahma, Pranagnihotra, Varaha, Kalisantarana, and Saraswati Rahasya;

those belonging to Samaveda – Kena, Chandogya, Aaruni, Maitrayani, Maitreyi, Vajrasuchika, Yogachudamani, Vasudeva, Maha, Sanyasa, Avyakta, Kundika, Savitri, Rudrakshajabala , Darsana, and Jabaali; and those belonging to Atharvana veda – Prasna, Mundaka, Mandukya, Atharvasirah, Atharvasikha, Brihadjabaala, Nrisimhapoorvatapini and uttratapini, Naradaparivrajaka, Sita, Larabha, Tripadvibhutimahanarayana, Ramarahasya, Ramapoorvatapini and uttaratapini, Sandilya, Paramahamsaparivrajaka, Annapoorna, Surya, Atma, Pasupathabrahma, Parabrahma, Tripuratapini, Devi, Bhavana, Bhasmajabala, Ganapathi, Mahavakya, Gopalapoorvatapini and uttaratapini, Hrishna, Hayagreeva, Datttareya, and Garuda.

Upanishads teach that everything is in the Self only. Everything else is nonexistent. A brief account of the essence of some of the important upanishads is given. Bhagavan Sri Sankaracharya has chosen ten Upanishads out of these 108 upanishads and felt that understanding these ten is sufficient as they contain the essence of all the remaining Upanishads and forms the basis for Hindu philosophy. He has written commentary for those Upanishads in detail. These ten Upanishads are selected here for brief presentation.

(i) Aitareyopanishad

This Upanishad belongs to Rigveda. Before this Upanishad, in the earlier three parts 'prana worship' was discussed. This worship leads to purification of mind. Then such a person becomes eligible to learn' Brahmavidya' the supreme spiritual knowledge. Then, the three subsequent parts of this upanishad assist the seeker achieve liberation. The first part contains three sections. There are four mantras in the first section and five mantras in the second section. The third section has fourteen mantras. The second part contains four sections. The first, second and the third sections contain one, two and one mantra respectively. While the fourth and the last section contain two mantras, the third and the last part contains only one section with four mantras.

In the first section of the first part, creation of the worlds and the rulers for worlds created was explained. All these worlds that are seen now were, before creation, one with 'Paramatma', the Supreme Reality. He desired to create the worlds. Then, he created first the worlds, Ambhas, Marichi, Maram and Apah. Ambhas (space) is above all. Below it is Marichi, the world of rays of light or illumination. Then maram is the earth where deaths occur. Below the earth is Patal or 'Apah'. The Lord then brought a lump from the waters and shaped it into 'purusha' in the form of man. This purusha was called Virat. Here waters mean all the five elements. He created Agni, Vayu and other rulers for these worlds. From the speech organ of the Virat, Agni manifested. From nose Vayu, from eyes sight, from his ears Directions (Dikpalakas) or

Quarters, from his hairs herbs, from his heart mind and from mind Moon and from his navel Apana, the Death, were created. From his generating organ semen and further from it water came into existence. In this way He created various rulers for the world he created.

In the second section, creation of places for the ruling gods was explained. The rulers so created fell into this world. They were afflicted with hunger and thirst. They requested the Creator to provide them with a place where they can live. He created several life forms such as horse, cow and others. But these devas did not find those forms satisfactory. Finally, when God created man, exactly as virat was, did the devas, the rulers of the world, agree to enter and take their positions. Agni entered through the mouth and became his speech. Similarly Vayu entered through the nose, sun entered through the eyes, Directions entered through the ears, Herbs and Plants entered through the skin, Moon entered into the heart, Death took its place at the navel while water entered into the generative organ. Hunger and thirst could not find places for them. When approached, God assigned them a share with every other ruling god in the body. Thus they get their share through the gods whenever sacrifices (havis) are performed.

The third section narrates the creation of food (annam). The Lord having created the worlds, and the rulers for these worlds, decided to create food for the people who live in these worlds. From water He created solid food, 'Annam'. All the gods tried to grasp the food but could not do so. Through sight, hearing power, touch or smell or any other sensing power it was not possible to consume food. Prana helped in digesting the food. The air (prana) that enters the body through the nose could enable the food to get digested and let off the undigested through the rectum and anus. Apana of Prana helps in this process. The Creator then thought that the 'pura' or the body of man so created would not be able to survive unless he himself stays within. Thus, He entered the Pura (city or human body) through the middle of the skull. His place in the wakeful state is the right eye, in the dream state the mind and in the sleep state the heart. He thus became Purusha in the Pura the body and falling into ignorance, thought that he is a worldly person. He realized with the grace of a guru or teacher that he is none other than the Creator Brahma himself.

In the second part the four sections explain the three stages of the jiva or soul. Man ejects semen into the woman. The self of the father enters into the mother and under the protection and care of mother and father the child is born. This is necessary to keep the world populated. The first stage of the jiva is to remain in semen, a lamentable situation. The second stage is to remain in the abdomen of the mother amidst faeces and urine, a highly detestable stage. The third stage is the old age when the body would get afflicted with several diseases and ultimately death occurs. The process of entering another body starts again, according to past actions and their results. All these three stages are abhorrent and disgusting.

There are five sheaths which enclose the jiva or the soul. They are the 'annamaya kosha' or the food sheath (physical body), 'pranamaya kosha' or the energy sheath, 'manomaya kosha' or the mental sheath, 'vijnanamaya kosha' or the knowledge sheath and 'anandamaya kosha' or the bliss sheath. These five sheaths encapsule the soul and keep it in ignorance. The realization of the Self and its nature enabled sage Vamadeva to break open these sheaths and obtain liberation. Man is encapsuled by these sheaths and maintained in ignorance or 'Maya'. He is entrapped into the cycles of birth and death eternally. Thus, contemplating on the self and by examining its nature one can obtain liberation as Vamadeva achieved.

In the third and final part it is emphasized that renunciation alone is sufficient for self realization. By examining one should notice that the body and its organs are not the self. Even the mind is not the self. Eyes can see. Ears can hear, skin can perceive touch. But, none of them experiences the sensations. The one who experiences the sight, the sound, the touch and other sensations is different. The sense organs are only implements and external. The power of the sense organs to see, hear, smell, taste and touch is a reflection of Virat, the universal person and ever dynamic life force. Consciousness exists at both heart and mind. Both are the reflections of Virat only. None of the manifested things can be the self. The adjunctless Self is pure and dynamic and observed through various 'upadhis' or objects of form. The witnessing dynamic life force is the true 'atma' that should be worshipped.

The Self is devoid of all adjuncts. Prana is Hiranyagarbha. He entered all the bodies. He is not different in different bodies. He reflects himself in all the bodies in their consciousness and organs of sensations, just as sun reflects in all water bodies. He is also Indra, the lord of all devas. Virat is the first person created. From him all the devas (Agni and others) manifested. They are his 'praja' or people. The five elements are responsible for all the bodies and he is all the five elements. Hiranyagarbha, Virat and Jivatma are all different but are the manifestations of pure consciousness. They are different from 'Eswar' the Supreme Lord.

This Upanishad ends with one of the famous 'Mahavakyas' or erudite sentences that summarize the vedic knowledge - "Prajnanam Brahma". Pure consciousness is Brahma. Individual soul is identical with Brahma.

(ii) Eesavasya Upanishad

This Upanishad belongs to Shukla (white) Yajurveda. It is concerned more with knowledge part or 'Jnana' and does not deal with karma or action aspect. There are 18 mantras or hymns in this Upanishad. They explain the crux of Hindu philosophy.

The whole universe is pervaded by Iswara, the Supreme Reality. Hence, enjoy this life with a feeling of sacrifice. Do not aspire for others' riches. Do constant selfless service to humanity. One must perform all the stipulated duties without expecting any benefit. Developing desire for liberation will gradually destroy all worldly desires.

The Supreme Reality called 'Parabrahma' is motionless and yet moves when associated with an object. It is all pervading. It is within all and outside all. It is swifter than mind, since it is Omnipresent. That is why, however fast the mind may contemplate and reach a distant object it will find 'Brahma' or 'Atma' already being present there. It is very nearer to an enquirer who understands it and is very far from the one who cannot conceive the truth.

The Self that is Atma is inside every one. It fills and covers everything. It is all full. It is the substratum of all beings. It is the subtlest inner self. The one who has realized the Self feels that all beings are not different from himself and sees himself in every being. He will not have any attachment and worries. He is completely freed from all dualities. He becomes fearless. He is freed from hatred, delusion and sorrows.

The knower is completely freed from ignorance, desire and action. This freedom is Jnana or self realization that the self has no body and is luminous transcendental, self sprung, and self existent. It is absolutely independent. Being Omniscient, the Supreme Reality – Brahma, ordains the fruits of one's Karma. Karma (actions, ritualistic duties) will not make one immortal. Moksha or freedom from birth and death cycles is obtained only through Jnana or knowledge of the Self. The supreme reality or Paramatma is the ear of the ear, tongue of the tongue, speech of the speech, life of the life and eye of the eye. While performance of karma leads to purification of mind and heart, understanding the self will make the wise immortal.

(iii) Taittiriyopanishad

This Upanishad is in three parts; each part is called a 'Valli'. In each part or valli there are several sections called 'Anuvakas'. The first part is called 'siksha valli' meaning chapter on instruction.

Siksha valli: Siksha valli deals with instructions about character and right conduct to the aspirants of learning so that they will become eligible to grasp the sacred knowledge of the Supreme Reality called Brahma vidya. Mitra, Varuna, Aryaman, Indra, Brihaspati, and Vishnu are invoked for granting welfare and bliss. There are six items considered for instructing the science of phonetics. They are vocalic sounds (varnas) pitch (swara), quantity (matra), force required for articulation (bala), modulation (sama), and joining of letters (Sandhana).

The doctrine of conjunction is explained with reference to the five perceptibe objects –the world, light, knowledge, progeny and self.

Earth below, firmament above are joined by atmosphere filled with air.

Fire and Sun give water and lightening joins them.

Teacher and pupil through the process of learning are united with knowledge.

Mother and father through the process of procreation produce the progeny.

Lower jaw and upper jaw through the function of vocal cords produce speech.

These are the five great combinations. One, who meditates on theses combinations will get food, cattle, progeny, wealth and other things needed for a happy life. Brahma the Supreme Lord is prayed for bestowing intellectual vigour and immortal elevation to the self.

Bhuh, Bhuvah and Suvah are the celebrated mystical sounds. A fourth sacred sound is Mahah, that is Brahma or Atma. All other gods are the limbs of Brahma. Bhuh stands for the world (Riks, fire, prana). Suvah stands for the heaven (Yajus, Vyana Aditya). Bhuvah is the intermediate space (Saama, Vayu, Apana). Maha is the solar plane (the moon, Pranava sound, food). These are called the four' Vyahrities'.

Worshipping on the bright space or cave in the heart, one may activate the Sushumna nadi that passes along the spine right up to the middle of the skull and thus create a path to the Supreme Lord. Meditation on Bhuh, Bhuvah, Suvah and Mahah leads to merger with Brahma. Through meditation on the five elements, the five sense organs and the five vital airs, the five fold principle of the nature can be understood.

Aum, the pranava sound is Brahma. Sages have become great by practicing right living, observing self denial, self restraint tranquility, and by following the rules ordained by the scriptures such as giving oblations, extending hospitality and general concern for human welfare. These are the high lights of Siksha valli.

Ananda valli or Brahmanandavalli

This part contains the two great quotations;

Brahmavidapnoti param - Self realized, attain liberation

Satyam, Jnanam, Anantam Brahma - Brahma is Truthfulness, Knowledge and Infinitude.

That Brahma is realized in the cave of the heart. From him emerged the sky, from sky air, from air fire, from fire water, from water food, and from food came all the beings.

All the beings on the earth are born from food and sustained by food. At the end they return to it. Food is the supreme and the first created. It is Atma. All creatures consume food and are consumed by food. Hence, it is called 'Anna'. This physical body can be conceived as self enclosed by a sheath called 'annamayakosha' or food sheath.

Following the upanishadic saying

Pranohi Bhutanaam Ayuhu – The life span of the beings depends upon Prana.

All the organs of men, animals and other beings are sustained by prana, the life force.

The Self considered as dependent upon prana is called 'pranamayakosha' or vital sheath. The annamaya kosha is permeated by pranamaya kosha. The pranamayakosha is further permeated by manomaya kosha, vijnanamaya kosha and anandamaya kosha or sheaths of mental, knowledge and bliss respectively. All these vital, mental and knowledge sheaths have the form of purusha or human. Mind is the embodied soul of pranamaya body. Intelligence is the embodied soul of the manomaya body. Sacrifices and various deeds are performed due to the power of knowledge sheath. By meditating on the knowledge body as the supreme, all sins can be got absolved and all the desires fulfilled.The knowledge body contains a self called Bliss or Ananda. It is also in the form of a person. It has love as its head, joy as its right wing, delight as its left wing, bliss as the trunk and Brahma as its basis. This Anandamaya kosha or bliss sheath denotes absolute delight. The happiness experienced by the realized persons at this stage is inexplicable.

Unless the Supreme knowledge is gained here and now in this birth, it is not possible to get it after the soul leaves the body.

Atma desired to become many and he projected all that exists now as universe. He is both the defined and the undefined. He is both the Established and the unestablished, the Consciousness and the Unconsciousness, and the Truth and the Falsehood. Whatever exists He is in it: so he is the Reality.

At the beginning there was Nonexistence and so Nonbeing. From that the Being emerged. He became the flavour of existence.

Out of fear of Him, the wind blows, Sun rises, Agni, Indra, Yama and other gods perform their duties.

The bliss experienced when the Supreme is realized is million million times greater than the joy experienced from sense objects. This is Brahmananda.

The soul that comprehends the nature of the Divine after departing from this world transcends Annamaya, Pranamaya, Manomaya, Vijnanamaya and Anandamaya Selves. He lives beyond right and wrong. He is one who found redemption.

Bhriguvall: Varuna explained the nature of Brahma to his son Bhrigu. Following the instruction of his father, Bhrigu after performing penance understands that all beings emerge from, are-sustained by and merge into food. On further enquiry about Brahma and on performing further austerities he finds that Prana the life force is Brahma as it sustains life and its exit causes death. But, still unsatisfied he approaches his father for further clarification. With the same advice repeated he performs further austerities and discovers that 'Manas' or mind is Brahma since beings are born from mind, sustained by mind and merge into mind. In the next stage of enquiry he finds that 'Vijnana' or knowledge is Brahma as beings are born out of knowledge, sustained by knowledge and merge into knowledge. Finally, by the same process

Bhrigu arrives at the conclusion that 'Ananda' is Brahma. All beings are born out of bliss, live in bliss and merge into bliss. This bliss is hide in the cave of the heart. He, who understands this is firmly established in it.

Life is food. Body eats it. Life is set in the body. Hence, food is set in food. He who knows this commands food.

Water is food. Fire is the eater of the food. Fire is set in water. Water is set in fire. Therefore food is set in food. He, who understands this commands food. He becomes great.

Earth is food. Sky is the eater of the food. Sky is established on earth. Earth is set on sky. Therefore, food is set in food. He, who knows this commands food. He becomes great.

Food should be given liberally. Food should not be refused. Householders should get food prepared for guests.

Food is the eater and the composer. It is the first born. He, who knows this achieves greatness.

The manner of worship of Brahma determines the nature of the return. If one meditates on Brahma as great, one becomes great. The one in the man and the one in the Sun are the same.

This is how the nature of the Absolute or Brahma is explained in this Upanishad.

(iv) Kathopanishad

This Upanishad belongs to Krishna (black) Yajurveda and is to be found in Charaka branch of Katha Brahmana. It teaches Brahma Vidya through a story.

There are two adhyayas or parts each with sub part called 'vallis'. There are three vallis in the first part and three vallis in the second part. In all, the first part contains 71 mantras and the second part 38 mantras.

Uddalaka, also called Vajasravasa a famous sage, once performed a great sacrifice. The sacrifice is called 'Sarvamedha' meaning sacrifice of everything. He donated every thing that he had in his possession. However, he kept back some cows that were giving plenty of milk for the sake of his young son Nachiketa. Observing that his father was donating cows that would not be useful at all to the receivers and good milk yielding cows were kept back, Nachiketa felt unhappy. In order to protect his father from falling into the den of sins, he repeatedly enquired from his father as to whom Nachiketa himself would be donated. Getting annoyed at the repeated enquiry from his son, Uddalaka replied that Nachiketa would be given to Yama the king of the nether world. Eventhough Uddalaka said this in a state of annoyance, Nachiketa was not willing to let the word of his father go invain. He left his father's home and proceeded to the city of Yama. When Nachiketa reached the place of Yama, Yama was not at home. Nachiketa waited at the door of his home three nights fasting all along. When Yama returned home he wanted to play host to Nachiketa. Since Nachiketa waited continuously for three nights, Yama decided to grant three boons to him. Yama told him to ask for the boons. Nachiketa desired that his father may not be angry with him for leaving for Yama's city and treat him well after his return from the city of yama.

Beings in Heaven live in peace. 'Agnividya', worship of fire is means to reach Heaven. Nachiketa wanted knowledge of Agnividya to be granted to him as the second boon. Granting this boon, Yama explained the complete procedure and the intricacies involved in this worship through fire. Nachiketa learnt the art with great ease. Satisfied with the performance of Nachiketa Yama granted him an additional boon. He declared that the form of worship through fire that was taught to Nachiketa would henceforth be called after Nachiketa. He also gave him a necklace of precious stones. The fire god worshipped is none other than Virat, born from Hiranyagarbha.

Overcoming death is the result of worship through fire. Discriminating power would be obtained. This enables one to give up attachments and enmity. Once ignorance vanishes the need for sacrifice does not arise. As actions are not performd intentionally the result of actions do not have any influence. This is overcoming death and rebirth.

Nachiketa desired to learn from yama 'Brahmavidya' or Self realization as his third boon. Yama dissuaded him, pleading that such subtle knowledge can not be given. Yama tried to persuade him in several way to seek any other material benefit rather than Brahmavidya. But, Nachiketa did not relent and Yama had to yield and give the knowledge of liberation.

In the second valli of first adhyaya, two paths of spiritual progress are explained. The first one is 'Preyas' which bestows on the person, children, cattle, wealth and others which are perishable or impermanent. The other part is 'Sreyas'. Very few would opt for this path. Nachiketa opted this path. Yama informed Nachiketa that he had become fit to receive 'Atmavidya'.

All penances, Upanishads, celibacy, yama, niyama and others contain the same as that, that exists in the prnava sound AUM. Only humans can achieve liberation. Only a discriminating intellectual who understands the distinction between ignorance and knowledge gets liberated. All actions are motivated by ignorance and result in materialistic wealth. This results in death and birth cycle. Atmavidya can be learnt from only a qualified teacher. Permanent soul can not be realized by impermanent means. The position of Hiranyagarbha is also impermanent. Knowledge of the Self annihilates attachments with the external world. AUM is the sound of the self. AUM is the symbol for the self. Aum is to be meditated upon as a representative of Brahma. Aum is Brahma. One who meditates upon Aum as Hiranyagarbha attains the state of Hiranyagarbha. If one understands Aum as the Supreme reality he attains that. That is the fruit of meditating on Aum. It is higher worship than Gayatri. Atma is ever present and unchanging. There is no difference between jeeva and brahma. They are the same. Ignorant persons think that body is Self. Atma is immortal. It is subtler than atom. It is grosser than the grossest.

" Anoraneeyan – Mahatomaheeyan"

Without this Self everything in the universe loses its power. It can be identified through hearing about it, meditating upon it and through such means. Mind should be withdrawn from the external objects. When mind gets stabilized, self will be realized.

Eventhough the self is inert, it travels to distant places. Moves in all directios. It contains all dualities. It can not be understood by study of scriptures. It can be realized only through intense meditation. Good character and control of senses are means for it. Pure consciousness at the times of creation, sustenance and dissolution takes the assistance of illusion, a product of balance, action and inertness. While dissolving the creation, it remains inert.

Body and sense organs are used by jeeva as horses and mind as reins, intellect as chariot driver. If intellect fails Atma can not be realized. The path to Atma is seen by a person with steady and pointed mind.

In the body, atma in the form of jeeva, eats the fruits of its own actions. Paramatma, the Supreme Lord does not participate in that. But, by virtue of his association Paramatma also participates. They are like the light and its shadow. One is experiencing while the other is not. Worldly life and liberation are two choices before jeeva. Depending upon the chariot driver the body chariot moves. Jeeva's journey in life depends upon the intellect and wisdom of the driver.

Senses depend upon the existence of the object for their functioning. The objects are dependent upon the mind that undergoes different impressions.Intellect controls the mind and hence is very important. The sum total of the intellect of all the beings is the mind of Hiranyagarbha and it is great. He is knowledge and action. The unmanifest (Avyakta) is much more than Hiranyagarbha. He is the seed for the whole universe. Realization of this Unmanifest annihilates death and birth cycle.

Elements are five in nature. Sound, touch, form, taste and smell are their characteristics. Earth has all the five characteristics. Water has no smell and hence has only four attributes. Fire has no smell and no taste. It is subtler than both earth and water. Air has no smell, no taste and no form. It has only the two remaining attributes. Ether or space has only sound in it. Atma which is subtler than everything else in the universe possesses no attribute at all. It is permanent and impermanent. It has no cause and no effect; neither beginning nor end. This knowledge leads to immortality. This atma is manifest in all beings. Persons who pursue it with single minded thinking can know this.

The obstacles are the sense organs. They have to be controlled. Desire for physical comforts and ignorance (Avidya) are the reasons. Attachments are obstacles and detachment is required. Once the Truth is realized there will be no more desires. The truth (Paratatva- the nature of the Supreme) is that which possesses the knowledge of both the wakeful world and the dream world. It is also the ruler of the past, present and the future. That ruler is none other than the self. Jeeva has actions and their results. Eswar is unlimited by time. Ignorance of jeeva causes action. Once this ignorance is removed the Divinity of the Self will be understood. Pratyagatma (the atma experienced) is seen as Paramatma. This Paramatma or Eswar is also ' Sarvatma.' Hiranyagarbha tatva or the nature of Hiranyagarbha exists in all the beings (sarvantara). He created the five elements. With the three properties of action, balance and inaction. Balance or Satva created Antahkarana. When this veil or Antahkarana is removed the unity between jeeva and Hiranyagarbha becomes apparent. This Hiranyagarbha is the life form of the supreme Reality or the Unmanifest. He has 'Lingasareera' and is thus called 'Prana'.

Virat is fire in sacrifice (Yajna). When meditated upon him in the heart, he is the agni or fire in the heart. This was revealed to Nachiketa.

All the gods including the sun are Hiranyagarbha only. The life force in the body is the Supreme Reality only. There is no difference. The only thing to know in this world is the nondistinction between jeeve and Atma.

In the cave of the heart there exists 'Antahkarana'. This acts as support to life force that fills the entire body as well as outside it. The Ruler of the worlds exists all times. He therefore exists in past, present and future.

The body has nine openings or gates. (two nostrils, two ears, two eyes, mouth, two openings of the excreting organs) and at the centre and top of the skull there is (brahmarandhra) through which Purusha entered the body. Atma or Purusha is the king of this body considered as a city or fort. Meditating upon Him leads to liberation. As atma is limited to the size of the thumb in the cave of the heart, He is called Vamana.

People obtain bodies that are consistent with their past actions. Even when all organs rest in sleep Purusha does not rest.

Eventhough fire is one of the elements the means for it are several. The most subtle atma is all pervading. Just as fire enters firewood, atma enters all bodies. Fire assumes the shape of round, long or circular according to the shape of the burning substance. In the same way atma assumes a form. Based on the birth, death, organ construction we see different jeevas but the atma is one and the same in all beings.

Ignorance creates desires. Desires create action which leads to unhappiness. Atma has no ignorance.

When dissolution occurs all the energy of the created beings enters into Atma. With this energy the cycle of creation starts again.

This world has its root at the top. That root is clean, pure dynamic, life sustaining Atma. Hiranyagarbha and others are its branches. The tree is everlasting. This Atma must be realized before the body falls. Like an image in mirror, pure mind reflects Atma. Yoga is the means to realize that atma.

Once "Aham Bramhasmi" is understood during one's own life, he overcomes death and becomes immortal.

This is the essence of 'atma vidya' explained to Nachiketa by Yama.

(v) **Brihadaranyakopanishad**

This Upanishad belongs to shukla Yajurveda. There are six adhyayas or parts in this Upanishad. This Upanishad contains the essence of all the Upanishads.

Adyaya 1: *Brahmanas* 1 and 2: Aswamedha sacrifice is the main topic of the first two brahmanas. The creator is invoked in the horse for worship. Dawn, daytime, night, lightning, space, sun, fire, and other such things are attributed to various parts of a horse. Those who consider the horse sacrifice as an act of self sacrifice become immortal and merge into Hiranyagarbha. This is called worship of prana (life force) or pranopasana.

Brahmana 3; Hiranyagarbha desired company after he was created from the Unmanifest. He felt lonely. Out of his own free will, he created a woman from himself called Satarupa. The male part that remained of Hiranyagarbha became Manu. Together they created all the living beings on earth. The last species to apper in the creation were humans. Apart from this story of creation this brahmana contains an important triplet of great spiritual importance.

"Lead me into that Reality from the untruth (world) "- **"Asatoma sadgamaya"**.

"Lead me into the light (of knowledge) from the darkness (of ignorance)" – **"Tamasoma jyotirgamaya"**

"Lead me into that supreme bliss from unhappiness" – **"Mrityorma amritangamaya"**.

Brahmana 4: The unmanifest from which the manifest world was created was compared to a tree. To get freed one has to cut this tree with knowledge and renunciation. Self (Atma) must be worshipped as the most dearest one. Self is Brahma. Out of ignorance one thinks that he is experiencing the pleasures and pains,. But in reality he is the Self (Atma) only. With this knowledge experiencing the self in every thing will be the outcome of self realization. Before creation there was one Manifest Brahma (Hiranyagarbha). But, after creation he manifested in everything.

Finite actions such as penance, sacrifice, and others can not result in unlimited benefits. Just as silk worm gets entangled in the silk threads that it weaves, so also man gets bound by the results of his own actions.

Brahmana 5: God created food (annam) for all the beings. One should not prepare food for himself; he should share with other beings. The adhibhoutika and adhi daivika aspects of mind, speech and life force are explained.

Brahmana 6: The prana or life force that entered into the name, form and action oriented physical body is immortal. Even if the body dies, it exists in the subtle form as a seed for future. In the same way even after the world ceases to exist it remains as a seed in the unmanifest world. Life force has no death. Prana is Amrita (ambrosia).

Adhyaya 2: *Brahmana* 1; Atma has to be realized. It has two facets. The internal one is the subtle form sustained by prana, immortal and selfluminous. The external one is the gross form. It is nonluminous, and has got the birth and death attributes. It is an external covering to the internal body that is ever living. This life force is common to all living beings. Its external is Virat, made of the five elements. Its head is the fire and its eyes are the sun and the moon. All actions are motivated by the life force. Hiranyagarbha has Virat as body in the universal plane.

Sage Gargya was of the opinion that Brahma is to be worshipped as the powers contained in the sun, the moon, electricity, air, fire water, reflected image in mirror, reflected sounds, shadows, space and intellect

Ajatasatru, a kshatriya king enlightened him about the nature of Brahma. All the characteristics inherent in the various items mentioned by Gargya are to be identified with the single entity 'prana'. It is awake even when one is asleep through breathing process. A sleeping person can not respond when addressed to Prana cannot be Brahma. All the organs of actions and senses along with prana exist only to help maintain the body. Brahma is the one who neither wanes nor waxes. He has neither birth nor death.

Brahmana 2; When prana is in the body, the body works. The two nostrils, the two eyes, the two ears and the mouth are the seven pranas and also the seven rishis. Gautama and Bharadwaja are the two ears,. Viswamitra and Jamadagni are the two eyes, Vasishta and Kashyapa are the two nostrils and Atri is the mouth. Speech is the eigth prana.

Brahmana 3: In the spiritual plane (adhyatma) manifest (moortha) is eye. Unmanifest (Amoortha) is prana. Prana belongs to subtle body. Eye belongs to gross body. Subtle body is important.

Brahmana 4: When sage Yajnavalkya wanted to give away all his worldly possessions to his two wives so that he can go and perform penance, Maitreyi, one of his wives refused wealth and wanted her husband to give her divine knowledge. Yajnavalkya explained that Atma is dissolved in the universe, just as salt gets dissolved in water. In the same way as the water tastes salty, Atma dissolved in the universe can also be experienced. Every bit of it contains its effulgence. Therefore if Atma is realized then the whole universe will be understood.

Brahmana 5: To understand this atma hearing of scriptures from masters, (sravana), reflecting on the teachings diligently (manana), and meditating with concentration (nididhyasana) is necessary.

Brahmana 6: When the lineage of masters is traced we end up with Hiranyagarbha. He had no master. He gained the Divine knowledge from the Supreme Reality (Parabrahma) due to His grace.

Adyaya 3: *Brahmana* 1: Once king Janaka was performing a great sacrifice. Several great scholars arrived to witness the sacrifice. Janaka decorated one thousand cows with gold and silk and declared that any one who could explain the Supreme Reality to the satisfaction of all in the assembly can take away the cows. A Brahmin called Yajnavalkya directed his disciples to take away the cows to his home. All the scholars in the court of Janaka got infuriated at this and challenged Yajnavalkya to prove his superiority over the rest.

Aswala put the first question. He wanted to know how a householder by performing a sacrifice can overcome death. Yajnavalkya replied in the following manner. Sun has no day and night. Sun's glory can be witnessed by the eyes only. By meditating on the sun and the eyes one can overcome the limitation of time and hence death. He also answered many other questions put by Aswala.

Brahmana 2: Another sage Arthabhaga put several questions about astronomy which Yajnavalkya answered well. He explained that after death while the body merges into the five elements the soul or spirit holds on to the fruits of the good and bad deeds performed by the person while he was alive.

Brahmana 3: To the question put by Bhujyuvu, Yajnavalkya explained that by performing the horse sacrifice (Aswamedha) one can reach the plane of Hiranyagarbha with the assistance of Vayu (air). In all the beings, movable and immovable, Vayu is inherently residing.

Brahmana 4: In reply to the question put by sage Ushastha, Yajnavalkya explained that other than all the organs of action and senses there exists an entity called 'atma' (self).

Brahmana 5: Sage Kahola wanted to know about 'atma' further. Atma is not influenced by any of worldly attributes such as hunger and thirst. It can be known only by renunciation. Brahmin is one who understands through the teachings of a master that he himself is the'atma' and there is nothing else other than the self.

Brahmana 6: Gargi wanted to know the location of the world of Brahma. Yajnavalkya replied that Brahma is the spirit that is inherent and holds everything in the universe together. He can be known only through Vedas.

Brahmana 7: In reply to a question by Uddalaka he explained that air is sustaining all the bodies and all the worlds. Air is present in waters. Air can be perceived through smell.

Brahmana 8: To another question from Gargi, Yajnavalkya informed that the universe is controlled and ruled by an ever existing reality that is dynamic, effulgent, and in which the whole unmanifest is present. This ever existing entity can see but, cannot be seen; can hear but cannot be heard; can know but, cannot be known and can think.

Brahmana 9: To a final question by sage Vidagdha, Yajnavalkya replied that there are three thousand three hundred and six devas or gods. But, important are only thirty three. They are:

Vasus 8: Agni (fire), Prithvi (earth), Vayu (air), Antariksha (sky), Aditya (sun), Dyulok (luminous space in the sky), Chandra (moon), Nakshatra (stars),

Rudras 11: Organs of action five and organs of senses five and mind.

Adityas 12: The twelve months in the year.

Indra: Parjanya or the source of rain, clouds.

Prajapathi: Yajna meaning cattle.

Yajnavalkya answered all the questions and justified his taking away the cows as gift from Janaka

Adhyaya 4: *Brahmana* 1: Later once again in the court of Janaka a discussion pertaining to Brahma took place. These discussions contained the following views:

Speech, prana, sound, mind, heart, vision or sight are all manifestations of Brahma.

Brahmana 2: Jeeva is Viswa in wakeful state, Taijasa in dream state and Prajna in sleep state. Atma exists in a state beyond these three states called Turiya.

Brahmana 3: Atma is self luminous. It is unaffected by the three states of existence.

Brahmana 4: Jeeva after death carries its impressions along with. It moves from body to body. It performs actions and from the results of these actions, builds body for the next birth. All actions are due to desires. A realized person does not perform actions with attachment to the results. Liberation is natural. Atma is without characteristics. The feeling of being different from atma is due to ignorance. Brahma alone is to be worshipped.

Brahmana 5: It is again Maitreyi brahmana. Yajnavalkya recommended to Maitreyi that hearing, reflecting upon what has been heard and meditating upon atma was the best method to attain liberation.

Brahmana 6 contains the lineage of teachers.

Adhyaya 5: *Brahmana* 1: The unique feature of pranava 'Aum' sound is explained. Aum is Veda. All the Vedas came out of that primieval sound. Brahma to be realized is Aum only.

Brahmana 2: Control over senses, charity, and kindness are the qualities to be possessed.

Brahmana 3: Brahma should be worshipped as heart (Hridaya).

Brahmana 4: Truth is Brahma; so should one worship Brahma.

Brahmana 5: The Truthbrahma has the sound 'Bhuh' as its head. The sounds 'Bhuvaha' are its hands. The sounds 'Suvaha' are its feet. 'Aham' is also a secret name for the 'atma' in the solar plane.

Brahmana 6: Brahma can be worshipped as the mind.

Brahmana 7: Brahma is also the electricity in the lightning.

Brahmana 8: Speech is also Brahma.

Brahmana 9: Vaiswanara, the fire in the digestion is also Brahma.

Brahmana 10: The worshipper will cross the air barrier and move to solar plane after death.

Brahmana 11: Even physical ailments such as fever should be considered as penance. Then one gets released from the past sins.

Brahmana 12: Food is Brahma.

Brahmana 13: Moving prana upward gives spiritual elevation after death.

Brahmana 14: The worship of Gayatri is said to make one immortal.

Brahmana 15: Agni (fire) is to be worshipped so that the soul is taken along a clear path towards heaven after death

Adhyaya 6: *Brahmana* 1: Prana is the most important of all powers in the body. One can live without being able to speak, hear, see, or even without being able to think in the absence of mind. But, without prana life does not exist.

Brahmana 2: The subtle body becomes a divine body in the luminous space above in the sky when appropriate sacrifices are performed during one's life time. The body liquifies and enters into clouds. Then as rain it returns to earth. Through the food stuff it enters into the man and into his semen. Then entering into the woman's womb body gets formed at the fifth stage. This is called 'Panchagnividya'.

Those who rely on works only reach the plane of the manes through the path of smoke, and then go over to the lunar plane and come back to take a new body. Those who do not perform any works and are carried away by jealousy and hatred will die on earth and take different bodies repeatedly.

Those who follw the path of renunciation and worship Hiranyagarbha travel through a clear and visible path to the plane of Brahma and will not return to earth.

Brahmana 3: A penance of twelve day duration for achieving great power (Mantha Karma), so that wealth comes through legitimate means for leading life in the world in a righteous manner is described.

Brahmana 4: The process of procreation and the birth of a child is described in this chapter.

Brahmana 5: In this concluding chapter the masters are praised and worshipped.

Thus, Brihadaranyaka Upanishad contains the essence of all the Upanishads and is considered very important.

(vi) Kenopanishad

There are four parts or Khandas in this Upanishad. In the first part there are nine mantras. In the second part there are five mantras. The third part contains twelve metered verses. Finally, the fourth part has nine mantras. This Upanishad belongs to Talavara Sakha

In the first part the nature of Brahma is explained in an inductive manner. At whose command does the mind work? Of all the things 'prana' the life force is the most important. At whose direction this prana is acting and performing its duties? At whose indication does the organ of speech talks? Which power is encouraging the eyes and the ears to perform their functions. These questions are answered thus: the supreme power that commands, directs and guides the various organs and even the life force, prana is called Brahma or 'Parabrahma' the Supreme reality or the Absolute Truth. It is the eye to the eye. It enables the eyes to see. It is the power that gives sight to the eyes. One who understands this attains immortality. It is only the power of Brahma that enables the organs of speech, sight, hearing, breathing and even the mind to perform their respective duties. Brave persons realize that they are not the perishable limiting adjuncts of the body but, they themselves are the pure immortal Brahma. Such people attain salvation or 'mukti'. The eyes cannot see Brahma. He is indescribable. He can not be grasped with the mind. He can not be understood by any known method. He is different from all that is known. He is different from that which is unknown. So, did the wise advise in the past. The power at the command of which the organ of speech can speak is Brahma. He can not be comprehended by any worship.

That Absolute can not be contemplated with the mind but, with Its' help and guidance mind can contemplate. It only should be worshipped.

That which can not be seen by the eyes but, gives sight to the eyes is Brahma. Know this. Any thing else is not worthy of worship.

That, which can not be heard but enables the ears to hear is Brahma. Know this.

That which can not be enlivened by prana, but gives life to the life force, prana is Brahma. Any thing else be not worshipped except that Brahma the Absolute and Supreme.

The five mantras in the second part explain further about Parabrahma and its' understanding. Brahma is not an issue of knowledge. Those who imagine that they understood the Absolute, indeed, have not understood Him. But, those who ascertain that they possess no knowledge of Him indeed, have realized Him.

"Avijnaatam vijaanataam vijnaatam avijaanataam."

The Self is embedded in the knowledge about everything. Vedic verses do not function as medicines to understand the Self. The seekers of the Self do understand the powers of the Self. This Self, none other than Brahma has to be realized here and now, in this birth. The Self exists in everything. Those who understand this become immortal.

The twelve verses of the third part establish the supremacy of Parabrahma over all other gods. At the time of war between the gods or devas and the demons, devas won the war over the demons with the blessing of the Absolute. However, the gods felt that the victory was only due to their own prowess. They became arrogant.

The Lord having observed them decided to teach them a lesson. He manifested before them in a brilliant and magnificient form. The devas were perplexed at the Divine form that stood before them. They sent Agni, the fire god to find out about the Divine Form. When the fire god went to the brilliant form, it enquired about him and the fire god told It that he can burn any thing with his power. The Magnificient form placed a piece of dry grass and asked him to burn it. Using all his power Agni failed to burn it. In a similar way Vayu, the wind god who went there later could not move the grass blade even a little bit with all his wind power. Then at the behest of all other gods Indra, the leader of all deities (devas) went to talk to the Divine form but, it disappeared. Then he went into meditation and prayed the Supreme Lord to enlighten him. The all merciful Almighty took the form of Parvati the divine consort of Lord Shiva and appeared before Indra. Indra prayed her to explain the Brilliant and Magnificient Form that they witnessed.

The nine verses of the fourth and the final part of the Upanishad contains the teaching of Brahma vidya or divine knowledge to Indra and the other two gods Agni and vayu.

She revealed that the victory of devas in the war against the demons was only dut to the power of Parabrahma. Infact, it was only the victory of the Absolute against the evil. Thus, Indra, Agni, Vayu and later all other gods obtained Divine knowledge from the goddess of Paravidya (Parvati).

Brahma is without comparision. When witnessed he appears a split second like a lightning. He must be deeply contemplated and then only he can be realized. The formless Absolute can not be understood by dull persons. Constant meditation about Brahma will enable such dull people slowly to understand the nature of the divine.

This Brahma is to be worshipped as it is the Self existing in all beings. It is sacred. With this feeling Brahma should be worshipped. Tapas or focused contemplation is a means for realization. Vedas, Vedangas and other scriptures, observance of truth, meditation are all means to attain the divine knowledge. The one who understands this is absolved of all the sins and is released.

Brahma is attained only by renunciation. Finite organs are made to function by Infinite Brahma. To define Brahma is to deny Brahma.

(vii) Chandogyopanishad

It belongs to Samaveda. There are eight chapters in this Upanishad. But, the knowledge part is contained in sixth, seventh and eighth chapters only. The earlier chapters deal with work part or 'karmakanda'. Strict adherence to performing one's own duty purifies the mind. Worship leads to mental steadiness. If cause and effect are different, then by investigating into the effect the cause can not be understood. However, if the cause and effect are the same, then by contemplating on the effect the cause can be realized. In the beginning there existed only one, the Absolute Reality. That Being willed and there was creation.

"Tadaikshat bahusyam"

That one became several. It created fire and from fire water was created. From water food came. Later life forms emerged. Some were born to eggs. Some came from living beings. And some other things came out of sprouts. That One Being called Brahma entered into the creation as Jeevatma or encapsulated soul.

Food when eaten gets divided into three parts. The grossest part that is taken is rejected as faeces. The middle part becomes flesh and the subtlest part mind. Water when taken in, becomes also divided into three parts. The grossest part is let out as urine. The middle part enters into blood. The subtlest part becomes prana, the life force. Fats (fire) that are taken in also are divided into three parts. The grossest ingredient becomes bone, the middle part turns into marrow and the subtlest part becomes speech. Thus mind is influenced by the food consumed. Water sustains life force, prana. Fire generated by fats influences speech or 'vak'. Thus the subtlest components are seen to be responsible for creation and this aspect is described as 'Anima'. It is also 'Atma' or Self.

Just as a bird tied to a string tries to fly away in different directions and fails to get freedom and settles down to its place, so also mind tied to prana tries to contemplate several things and ultimately takes refuge in prana. This implies that the encapsulated soul, jeevatma, after pursuing various worldly materialistic pleasures, ultimately recognizes the futility of the effort and takes refuge at the feet of the Almighty. True happiness is obtained only through self realization. In fact, this happens everyday in mans' life when he enters into the state of deep sleep. During sleep all the senses merge into the self. On waking up, the mind and the senses continue their work. In the same way, death is only a transition for the soul or jeevatma to continue the works left unfinished in the previous birth. Death is a transition for jeevatma in as much as sleep is a transition to living body.

By contemplating and analyzing things one can know the Truth or 'Sat'. Mind is greater than speech, while will is greater than mind. But, intelligence is greater than will and contemplation is greater than intelligence. Understanding is greater than contemplation and strength is greater than understanding. From food one becomes strong. Water produces food. Fire (heat or tejas) causes rain and water. The sources of fire, sun, moon, stars and lightning are all enclosed in Akash or ether. By such reasoning memory, hope and prana one can come to the conclusion that prana is the greatest thing without which no life can exist. An insight into the Absolute Reality is possible by constant contemplation till the goal is reached and then, one understands the Self. This whole universe is pervaded by Sat also called Bhooma. With the help of a Guru or teacher the seeker should arrive at the Truth, the Self.

Thou art that. *"Tat Twam Asi"* !

That self is not different from the one who is investigating.

(viii) Mundakopanishad

This Upanishad belongs to Atharvana Veda. It is in three parts. Each Mundaka contains two chapters.

The first chapter of the first part of Mundaka consists of nine verses. Hiranyagarbha was the first among the Gods. His first son was Atharva or Atharvan. Hiranyagarbha taught his son Atharva 'Brahmavidya' or knowledge about the Absolute Reality. Atharva taught this to Angira. He in turn explained this knowledge to Satyavahu. From Satyavahu Angirasa obtained this Brahmavidya. Saunaka a reputed householder approached Angirasa and requested him to teach this knowledge. Thus, this Upanishad is composed as a narration by Angirasa to Saunaka.

Knowledge is of two types 'para' and 'apara' or knowledge to understand and reach the Divine and the one that is good to lead the worldly life. All the information contained in the Vedas and related scriptures called Sikhsa, Kalpa, Vyakaran, Chandas, Nirukta, and Jyotish belong to apara vidya. This knowledge will not lead to Self realization or 'Mukti'.

The Absolute or 'Parabrahma' can not be comprehended with the sense organs. It has no eyes and no limbs. It is eternal, omnipresent and omnipotent. It is subtler than any subtle thing. Such an Absolute Reality is the basis for the existence of the whole world.

Just as a spider weaves a cobweb using resources from within its own body, so also Parabrahma created the whole universe out of Himself without any external assistance. The whole plant kingdom springs out of earth and hair comes out of living bodies. In the same way the world has come out of Hiranyagarbha. The great Parabrahma went into meditation, expanded and created the Unmanifest. From Unmanifest Hiranyagarbha was born. From Hiranyagarbha the Cosmic Mind came into existence. From the Cosmic Mind the five basic elements (pancha bhutas) were created. From these the whole of the universe was generated. Into the created world, life was brought in. In this way living beings , their actions to survive and the fruits of these actions came into existence. Thus, from the great Eternal Reality, who is the embodiment of knowledge Hiranyagarbha, all the seen world and food were created.

In the second part of the first Mundaka there are thirteen verses. These verses discuss the benefits of para and apara knowledge. Apara is connected with life and para is related to salvation. This part of the Upanishad instructs that rituals prescribed in Vedas must be performed. Sacrifices into the fire, honoring the guests and sacrifices connected with full moon and new moon should be performed. The seven flames of fire god are mentioned. The sacrifices will carry the performer to heaven through the rays of Sun god.

The fruits of sacrifices performed will lead to temporary enjoyment in higher worlds. But, thereafter the soul must return and undergo the cycle of births and deaths

People who feel proud of their scholarship and knowledge of scriptures are like the blind who can guide neither themselves nor others. Performing sacrifices, observing all rituals are helpful in gaining material benefits in this world but do not elevate the soul to avoid the cycle of birth and death. Performing actions to achieve happiness and fulfill desires will only degrade the soul. The purpose of life is to perform all actions without anticipating any fruits. All the sense and work organs must be controlled, celibacy should be observed and happiness and sorrows, both, must be renounced. Still, it may be possible to reach the plane of Hiranyagarbha, which is not liberation. Having performed all actions, one must realize that it is only through guidance of a Self realized teacher (Guru) that one can obtain the Divine knowledge and achieve liberation.

In the first part of second Mundaka there are 10 verses. They explain that from the immortal Brahma all the living beings emanated like the sparks from a blazing fire. Just as the sparks return to the same fire so also all the living again return to Him. The self luminous, all pervading and indestructible Brahma is shapeless, birthless and devoid of both prana and mind. Yet, He is the source to all life, mind, organs and all the five elements. From the first born Hiranyagarbha the cosmic person Viratpurusha was born with Sky as his head, sun and moon as eyes, directions as ears, Vedas as speech, and universe as his heart. He is the innate soul of all the living beings. Earth was born out of his feet.

Sun is the source of light in the sky. Moon is the source for the clouds. Clouds are the source for herbs on earth (through rains). From herbs man gets energy and ejects semen into the womb of woman, who is the source of creation.

From Vedas sprung all the sacrifices, rituals, time, householder, all sorts of works and the fruits of those actions. Sun and moon illuminate these worlds. From this Virat all the gods, vasus, sadhyas, men, cattle, birds, breaths, austerities, celibacy, modes of performing actions were created. The seven pranas, namely, two ears, two nostrils, two eyes, and the tongue, are born from him. Also, seven flames, seven fuels, seven oblations, seven seas and the seven worlds wherein the seven pranas move were created. Seven is a unique number. He lives in the inner self encircled by the five elements.

The world of knowledge and action were born from him. He resides in the cave of the heart. He, who understands the knot of ignorance is the liberated soul even while living in the physical body. He who realizes is verily the Brahma and becomes immortal.

The second part of second Mundaka contains 12 verses and it describes the method for realizing the Self (Atma). The Supreme is both gross and subtle and is the whole universe. It can not be comprehended through any of the worldly methods. It is brilliant. Subtler than an atom and yet, in it contained the whole world. One must center his mind in Him. Making the primal sound pranava AUM, as bow, and using mind as arrow, Brahma should be targeted. Since, jiva is in mind when the arrow, that is, jiva strikes Brahma, jive merges into Iswara the Supreme Lord. The seeker of Brahma becomes Brahma himself. Just as the spokes of a chariot wheel spread out from the center, the nadis (nerves) that manifest through the body are centered at the heart. Brahma, residing at the heart is a witness to all the mental activities. By Meditating upon AUM, under the guidance of an able teacher, ignorance can be overcome and the Self realized.

Brahma is the nature of the mind. He is brilliant, glorious and lives in the heart of all living beings. The gross and the subtle are both his forms only. He is subtler than the subtlest and grosser than the grossest. He is the life force, speech and mind.

All the doubts cease to exist once the knot in the heart is broken. The actions and their consequences exist in three modes, sanchita (results on hand), prarabdha (past action results now on hand) and agami (results to be experienced later). Sanchita and agami can be neutralized but, prarabda must be experienced.

Just as a sword is coverd by a sheath so also is Brahma enveloped by five sheaths. They are the food sheath or annamaya kosha, life sheath or pranamaya kosha, mental sheath or manomaya kosha, knowledge sheath or vijnanamaya kosha and bliss sheath or anandamaya kosha. Brahma the Supreme is the Atma inside the bliss sheath. This Atma is self illuminating and glorious. It is

Omniscient and exists in all the ten directions. Once the veil of ignorance gets removed, Brahma is seen in all and every thing.

The first part of third Mundaka consists of ten verses. In this part the body is compared to a tree. Two birds live on this tree. One bird eats the fruits of the tree while the other bird just watches without any action. The first bird is the jivatma which eats the fruits of its own action. The second bird which is the pure Self or Paramatma is a witness without any involvement. Following the path of yoga under the guidance of a teacher jiva overcomes ignorance and realizes that there is only one bird. The seer will then behold the golden coloured creator of the universe, Purusha, the source of Brahma. Once, realization of the Self occurs, identifying the self as Brahma materializes. The seer will see the same self in everything.

The self effulgent soul is seated in the heart. He can be contemplated by controlling anger and following the path of truth. Observance of Truth widens the Divine path and enables the person to reach 'Satya loka', the world of Truth.

Brahma is beyond description. He is untouched by actions. Organs have no effect. He is absolutely pure. Knowledge is the only path to reach Him. Truth is the means. With pure conscience and stable mind the Self illuminating Brahma can be realized in one's own heart. Such seers can obtain whatever they desire. They can also fulfill the desires of others.

The second part of third Mundaka includes 11 verses.'

Aksharaparabrahma' the Immortal Absolute contains the whole universe. The realized person can witness Him. The first requisite for realization is renunciation of all desires. The spirituality needed can not be obtained from knowledge of scriptures, nor by intelligence. It is obtained by intense desire and concentration. Once the Self is realized, oneness with the universe is attained. Just as all the rivers lose their identity once they merge into the sea, so also the seer will see Self in everything in the world.

(ix) Prasnopanishad

This Upanishad belongs to Atharvanaveda. Mundakopanishad is considered as a "mantropanishad". It explains the nature of 'Brahma' in a concise way. Prasnopanishad explains elaborately the same and hence is considered as a "Brahmanopanishad" for Mundaka. This Upanishad is in the form of questions put by the seekers of 'Brahmavidya' and answers by the master. There are in all six questions and hence six chapters in the Upanishad.

There are sixteen mantras in the first chapter. Six sages Sukesa, Satyakama, Sauryayani, Aswalayana, Bhargava and Kabandhi wanted to acquire Brahma vidya or knowledge about the Absolute Reality. They went to a great master Pippalada and requested him to teach them abou the Parabrahma the Absolute. Pippalada wanted them to observe celibacy for one complete year and come back to him. After one year they returned to him observing celibacy as stipulated.

Kabandhi wanted to know abut the process of creation. This was the first question. Pippalada explained: God contemplated and decided to create. He created a pair, matter and life. The pair is also called Rayi and Prana or Soma and Agni. Prana stands for Aditya, the Sun god. Prana eats food and Agni consumes everything. Rayi indicates the planet moon that contains matter, and food is also matter. Hence Agni, Aditya and Prana are all one and the same. So also, Rayi, food and matter or Moon are the same. It is implicit that the eater and the eaten create various creatures.

Aditya is also Prajapati or Patriarch. He is of the nature of time. He creates the equinoxes. His path of northward journey and later southward journey divides the year into two parts, 'Uttarayana' and 'Dakshinayana', the two 'Ayanas'. His movement also creates the day and night.

Persons who follw the path of action (karma) performing sacrifices and rituals will after their death reach the moon following the path of Dakshinayana and return to earth to take next birth. Those who seek 'Atma' with faith and knowledge reach the sun through the path of Uttarayana. This place is called' Brahmalok' and is the highest desirable place to live along with immortals.

The seasons are Aditya's feet. The seven colors are his horses. Also, the ayanas, ritus (seasons), months, pakshas(fortnights), days, nights and muhurtas are also considered as his seven horses. Prajapati is prana during the day time and Rayi, the moon for the night. Hence celibacy should be observed during the day. Observance of celibacy, truth and penance will enable one to reach 'Brahmalok'. One should give up falsehood, crookedness and fraud. Then only, after death one will follow the path of Uttarayana to Brahmalok.

The thirteen mantras of the second chapter answered the second question put by Bhargava. It was about the sustainers of the body and their greatness. Bhargava, a resident of Vidarbha, also wanted to know the greatest among the sustainers. Pippalada explained:

The five elements, earth, water, fire, air, and eather, the five sense organs eyes, ears, nose, tounge and skin and the five organs of action speech, hands, feet, and the two excretory organs are sustaining the body. Each of them boasted that the body is sustained only and solely due to their own power. Prana admonished them and informed that by prana splitting itself into five components (prana, apana, vyana, udana and samana) the body is maintained in a healthy state. The others did not believe this. Then, prana decided to leave the body as the other contenders did not agree. As prana prepared to leave, the body swooned and all the elements and organs of the body lost their power. They realized the power of prana and begged it not to leave the body. They praised prana stating that it s Agni(fire), Vayu (air), Parjanya (cloud), Surya (sun), and Indra (ruler of all gods). Prana is responsible for the existence of all the worlds. All the Vedas are in Prana. It is Prajapati. All the gods receive their share of sacrifice through Prana. Prana is 'Easwar', the creator, sustainer and destroyer. The capacities of the sense organs to see, smell, speak, taste and touch are due to Prana. Prana is the Supreme Prajapati.

A third question was put by Aswalayana Kausalya to Pippalada. It concerned the nature and origin of Prana. He wanted to know the origin, the purpose, the mode of entry, the way it exists, and its exit from the body.

Pipplada explained: Prana is the shadow of Paramatma and thus is not different from Him. Prana intends and does works to achieve them. To experience the fruits of the actions it takes birth in a body. Prana governs the body. Prana and apana enable the body to digest the food consumed. At the navel prana and apana balance and become 'samana'. In the heart 'jiva' lives. Heart is the centre for 'nadis'. One hundred of them start from the heart and each again splits into one hundred which in turn split further into seventy two. In addition an important nadi called 'Sushumna' also starts at the heart. It is directed upwards. Along with it moves udana part of prana. Udana helps in swallowing of food. From head to toe moving in the body, Prana dictates the destiny of the soul after the death of the body.

Prana in the external world is the Sun god. He bestows Prana and sight. Earth assists in the action of apana which is excretion of food undigested Vyana does the circulation of blood. The exit of Prana from the body causes death. Udana takes 'jiva' out of the body at the time of death. Whatever the jiva in the subtle body (lingatma) contemplates that will be the one with which Prana moves further and takes the next birth in another body. He, who knows the origin, the entry, the place of living, and the five fold distribution of Prana in the body becomes immortal. Thus, answer to the third question was given by Pippalada.

The fourth question was put by Sauryayana of garga clan. He wanted to know the organs that sleep and take rest and the organs that remain awake and perform their duties. He also wanted to know the organs that dream and rejoice them. He further wanted to know the place to where all the organs retreat during sleep. Pippalada explained:

The sun's rays emerge from the rising sun and retract back to him when he sets. But, on the next day when he rises again the same rays reappear. In the same way, while the person sleeps all the sense and work organs retreat into the mind. During sleep prana, apana and vyana vital airs work like the three sacred fires (tretagni). Samana sets the inhalation and exhalation in proper order. It is the powerful mind that dreams. Mind experiences dreams due to its past actions and impressions retained. The mind itself is the perceiver and the perceived. When a person gets enlightened he will dream no more.

In the deep sleep the causal body is active. It alone enjoys the happiness of deep sleep. The 'jiva' rests in Paramatma in deep sleep. with a thin layer of ignorance in between. In Samadhi state this layer of ignorance vanishes and the unity is complete.

Just as birds reach at the end of the day their respective nests or places of rest, so also, everything in the universe at the end merges with the Divine Spirit.

Mind is composed of manas, budhi, chitta and ahamkara. Manas or mind is that which cogitates (thinks). Budhi (intellect) is the discriminative faculty. Chitta is the reflexive mind or the faculty of memory. Ahamkara is the feeling of the self. The image of Brahma is reflected in all, in the same way as sun's rays get reflected in water. Brahma is formless, free from attributes, eternal and incomprehensible. He is the Supreme Bliss.

Satyakama, son of Sibi asked the fifth question through which he wanted to know the implications of meditating with the pranava AUM.

Aum is the symbol of Brahma. The mind of the meditating person should be steady like the flame of a lamp in windless place. Meditating on each syllable of the pranava gives different benefits. Only on the syllable A, if one meditates he will enjoy benefits on earth with all riches in the next birth. Meditation on the syllable U will take the jiva to the moon where it enjoys, but returns to earth thereafter. If one meditates on all the syllables of pranava together he will reach Hiranyagarbha at the solar plane. The three matras when contemplated separately are mortal but, together they lead to Divine Consciousness. In this way Pippalada explained the supremacy of meditating the pranava AUM as one word.

Sukesa of Bharadwaja clan wanted to know from Pippalada the nature of the person with sixteen kalas or parts. This was the sixth question. Pippalada informed him that he is none other than the Purusha who created Hiranyagarbha, Sradha, five elements, ten organs, food, semen, mantras, actions and all the worlds. All the sixteen kalas evolved from Him and are also within Him. It is by contemplation one should undetstand that the Purusha is one and only one without any parts (indivisible). He who knows that the kalas are attributed to Him in the same way as the spokes of a wheel are centered does not fear death.

Pippalada informed them that this is all that he knows and there is nothing further to know beyond this.

(x) Mandukyopanishad

This upanishad belongs to Atharvana Veda. There are only 12 mantras or metered verses in this upanishad and these twelve contain the summary of the whole vedic philosophy.

It explains the supremacy of prnava the primieval sound AUM. It stands for everything in the universe. All, that is past, present and future is included in AUM. Beyond the concept of these triple entities lies 'Turiya' state which stands for the Absolute called 'Brahma'. The primieval sound of vibration from which the whole universe is generated is AUM. The universal soul, Brahma, manifests in four states or stands on four 'padas' or legs.

The first 'pada' (leg) or state is 'Wakeful state' or 'Jagradavastha'. In this state the soul is called 'Vaiswanara' or universal person. He grasps the world through the five senses sight, sound, touch, smell and taste. For this he has 19 faces which are the five sense organs – ears, nose eyes, skin and tongue, five work organs – mouth, hands, legs and the two excretory organs, the five vital airs prana, apana, vyana, udana and samana and the four aspects of the mind or 'antahkarana', called mind, intellect, reflexive mind chitta, and ego. This universal man has seven organs. The glorious heaven is his head. Sun and moon are his eyes. Air is his breath. Space is his body. Water is his urinary organ. Fire is his mouth. Earth constitutes his feet or support. He is also called Virat. This Virat or Vaiswanara is the first quarter of the supreme Iswara. He is the macrocosmic aspect of the Omnipresent

Brahma. Vaiswanara in the microcosmic aspect is the individual soul or jiva.

The second state of existence of the individual soul is called Taijasa. He also has seven organs like Vaiswanara. He experiences dream objects in dream state. For this, he utilizes his own light. Infact he himself is that light. While in wakeful state Vaiswanara utilizes the light from the Sun, fire and such other sources, Taijasa creates objects from within and experiences them.

The third state of existence, the deep sleep state is experienced by the individual soul and in this state it is called Prajna. In this state all the senses merge into the individual soul and take rest and experience the bliss.

Beyond these three states is the fourth state 'Turiya', a state that can not be described by any sound or word. It can be conceived as absolute silence that is indescribable with any sort of adjuncts. It is the most blissful state with no attachments what so ever. The jiva or the individual soul thus exists in four different states.

When the sound 'A' is pronounced jiva remains in complete wakeful state.

When the sound 'U' is uttered the mind enters almost a dream state.

Finally uttering the sound 'M' leads the jiva into a state of sleep.

The fourth state 'Turiya' is absolutely soundless and prolonging the silence leads to 'nirvikalpa Samadhi' (super conscious state). If the individual soul or jiva is the physical body then, the sum total of all the physical bodies constitutes Virat. The sum total of all the subtle (sukshma) bodies is Hiranyagarbha. The aggregate of all karana or causal bodies is Iswara. The physical, astral and causal bodies are thus associated with Viratpurusha, Hiranyagarbha and Iswara.

In the wakeful state the physical body enjoys the worldly objects through the sense organs. In the dream state the astral body enjoys the dream objects which are its own creation. In the sleep state the casual body merges with Iswara and enjoys the bliss that is, Prajna in casual plane which experiences the happiness. Since mind is not functioning, egoism is not present in this state. This is a state of ignorance.

It is in the turiya, the state beyond the three states, the state of transcendental consciousness that the individual experiences absolute bliss having attained the knowledge of Brahma getting over the veil of ignorance.

CHAPTER 9

Vedangas

To spell, recite and comprehend the Vedic hymns and Vedic texts correctly, six other disciplines were created and they are treated as vedangas or the body organs of Vedas.

They are as follows:

1. Sikhsa

It deals with phonetics that includes pronunciation and accent. This includes the various ways such as mula, pada, krama, jata, and Ghana modes of reciting pathas. Maharshi Panini is credited for the development of this discipline. When one desires to express an object his mind reacts and body heat is produced. This directs the wind inside the body to move to regions of chest producing a low and mild sound. As it moves to the neck region, then to the head and ultimately to the mouth where it is heard as sound. Siksha refers to three different sound volumes - 'Udatha', 'Anudatha' and 'Swaritha', that is, high, low and medium respectively. Also, sound is differentiated on the basis of time over which it is uttered, viz.' Hraswa', 'Deergha' and 'Plutha', that is short, long and medium respectively. This science also identifies 8 places within the human body from where the sound accentuates. The manifestation of different syllables (aksharas) from these different locations and the times for the different syllables and their combination is described. A complete and thorough study of Vedas requires an in depth knowledge of Siksha sastra.

According to Tony Nader Ram* "Siksha is represented by structures which compute and express the internal aspects of physiology such as its biochemical constituents, temperature, pressure etc. These expressions are channeled via the autonomic ganglia. There are thirty six such channels on either side of the spinal cord. Correspondingly there are 36 books of Siksha."

(*Human Physiology: Expression of Veda and Vedic Culture. By Prof Tony Nader Ram).

2. Vyakarana

This is Sanskrit grammar. All the rules are laid down by Maharshi Panini so that by understanding these principles one can comprehend the true meaning of vedic verses. Unless one masters the rules of vyakarana it is not possible to understand the very subtle inner meanings of vedic mantras. The earliest work on vyakarana is due to Sakatayana (8 century B.C.). Based on his work Yaska (5-6 century B.C.) explained that a large number of nouns were derived from verbs through a derivation process. It became to be known as 'krit-pratyaya'. But, the work of Sakatayana is completely lost. Panini, (ca. 4. century B.C.) has done an extensive analysis of the processes of phonology (the sound system of a specific language), morphology (internal structure of the words), and syntax (rules of a language that show how the words of that language are to be arranged to make a sentence in that language.). Panini's grammar consists of four parts.

(a) Sivasutra : Phonology

(b) Ashtadyayi : Morphology, construction rules for complexes

(c) Dhatupatha : lists of roots. Classes of verb roots

(d) Ganapatha : Lists; classes of primitive nominal stems

Tony Nader Ram* identifies Vyakarana with Hypothalamus in human Physiology "Hypothalamus releases factors that activate the pituitary gland, neurohypophysis and autonomic nervous system. This represents expansion, fundamental to the process of evolution of the endocrine and autonomic response which leads to a large number of biochemical and physiological responses that bring the system to a new state of balance."

3. Nirukta

It is the science of the origin of the words and their development.

It comprises of the philosophy of etymology. Etymology is the study of the history of words. The source of the word as to how it is formed and the various aspects of its meanings are dealt with in this science. This sastra is due to sage Yaska (5-6 century B.C.). Nirukti noun in Sanskrit language means 'derivation' or 'artificial explanation of a word.' Quite often certain words will have hidden meaning. For example, the word Gananatha is understood to be Gana + natha (meaning protector of a group). A great scholar Bhaskara Raya explained it as Ganana + atha meaning the one, the enumeration of whose qualities bring auspiciousness. The word atha is associated with auspiciouness or 'mangalam'. Rhetoric skills in the art of Nirukta are considered as an asset to a commentator.

In the physiological mode of Tony Nader Ram Nirukta it is represented by pituitary gland, neurohypophysis and Sympathetic and Parasympathetic system. "It highlights the self referral direction involved in structuring Rigveda. These are activated by the limbic system and hypothalamic releasing factors. They expand the response and bring it back towards the organs and organ system of the physiology through a feedback loop that maintains the homeostatic balance."

4. Kalpa

This discipline is developed by several rishis. It contains the procedural rules for various rituals. The sacrificial practice of vedic culture gave rise to a large number of systematic sutras or codified laws for several classes of priests.

Kalpasutras: These are the rules of ceremonial rituals which can be classified further.

Shrautasutras: They are based on Sruti or veda. They teach the rules and regulations for the performance of great sacrifices. These sacrifices need three sacrificial fires.

Smrtasutras: These rules are based on Smrti or tradition. These can be further subdivided into Gryhyasutras and Dharmasutras.

Grhyasutras: They are domestic rules, that is, family rites such as marriage, childbirth, naming çeremony and others. These all ceremonies are performed in a simplified manner in the premises of the home with offerings in the domestic fire.

Dharmasutras: They deal with customs and temporal duties. They are the source for later law books. While srauta explains the different rituals of sacrifice, gruhya is concerned with domestic life. Ethics, laws and customs pertain to dharma (right conduct). These guide-lines are codified as sutras.

Shrautasutras of Yajurveda have a set of Sulba sutras, meaning the rules of the cord. Measurements' by cords for the construction of different types of altars for sacrifices are subject matter of these sutras. It will be interesting to note that the word geometry is derived from the two Sanskrit words 'jya' and 'miti'. Jya means earth and miti means measurements. Jyamiti is evolved to measure the dimensions for sacrificial places.

Kalpa sutras also define eight universal values (samanya dharmas) or atma gunas, viz. compassion, patience, freedom from jealousy, purity or cleanliness, not being obstinate, keeping a cool mind, non-covetousness, and renunciation.

In the physiological model of Tony Nader Ram, "Kalpa is represented by the structures that process and transform any specific or point value of expression into a response that takes into consideration the totality of physiological expressions. This is to be compared to the limbic system in physiology that plays the role of transforming any point value of expression into an expanded response which generates an adaptive adjustment of the physiology to maintain overall balance and homeostasis."

5. Chandas

Meter dealing with prosody is called chandas. It has been already pointed out that there are seven meters that are used for chanting or singing of Vedas. It is said:

" Chandah Pado Vedasya "

meaning that vedic meters are supported by chandas. Each vedic mantra or hymn has four padas. The basic meters contain several syllables per pada.

Gayatri chandas has 6 syllables in each pada, which make a total of 24 syllables.

Usnik chandas has 7 syllables in each pada, which make a total of 28 syllables.

Anushtubh chandas has 8 syllables in each pada, which make a total of 32 syllables.

Brihati chandas has 9 syllables in each pada, which make a total of 36 syllables

Pankti chandas has 10 syllables in each pada, which make a total of 40 syllables.

Trishtubh chandas has 11 syllables in each pada, which make a total of 44 syllables

And Jagati chandas has 12 syllables in each pada, which make a total of 48 syllables.

There are many more types which are complex in nature requiring great expertise in composing the hymns. Indravajra, Upendravajra, Bhujangavijrumbhita, Sragdhara are some of the complicated types. Adi Sankara has composed Soundaryalahari in Sikharini chandas that has 17 syllables in each pada. Chandas sutras are proposed by Pingala and based on these rules chandas sastra has emerged.

In the context of human physiology, "Chandas is found within the feedback loops of the hypothalamic pituitary axis and sensory – motor system. These are the resetting mechanisms that maintain proper balance within the range of transformation anticipated or ordained by the body" according to Tony Nader Ram. They maintain proper rhythm or meter. Tony Nader opines that Chandas in physiology is the measuring and quantifying quality.

6. Jyotish

Jyotish is said to be the eye of vedapurusha as with the knowledge of this science one can look into the past, present and future. Jyoti means light or light giving body. All heavenly bodies also give light. Hence, the science that deals with the heavenly bodies is called Jyotish sastra. It is the ancient Indian system of astronomy and astrology. The sun god is believed to have revealed this science to Maya, the architect. In this science the influence of nine planets, 27 stars, 12 bhavas and 12 rasis are considered Esoterically, it represents that human quality of self referral consciousness which sees the past, connects to the present and foresees the future, which is the quality of Seer or Rishi.

Suryasidhanta: Sage Narada is associated with this science. This science is further developed by sage Garga. While astronomy is concerned with movement of stars, planets and other heavenly bodies, astrology predicts the influence of the movements in the conduct of human affairs.

Varahamihira wrote 'Brihat Samhita' and Aryabhatta wrote 'Aryabhatteeya Sidhanta'

At a much later date Bhaskaracharya wrote 'Sidhanta Siromani'.

These works contain arithmetic, algebra, trigonometry, and geometry. and are applied to astronomical calculations.

The branch 'Sidhanta' of Jyotish deals with Indian astronomy, while 'Samhita' is concerned with mundane astrology and electional astrology. A third category of this science is called 'Hora' which is predictive astrology. Some scholars consider Jyotish sastra as consisting of six kinds of applications

Gola : Positional astronomy.

Ganita : Mathematical diagnostic tools for analyzing the resullts of Gola.

Jataka : Natal astrology.

Prasna : Answering specific question based upon the time, the question is asked.

Muhurta: Selecting an auspicious time for an event.

Nimitta : Omens and portents.

Several great rishis Vasishta, Bhrugu, Garga and others were masters of this sastra. Befor the present Kaliyuga began in 3102 B.C. sage Parasara, wrote an important book on Jyotish called, 'Brihad Parasara Hora Sastra '. He was the last rishi to be associated with this sastra. Later, Satyacharya and Varahamihira wrote books on Jyotish. Indian Jyotish relies on sidereal zodiac while the Western science uses tropical zodiac. Some other scriptures in Jyotish satra that are important are 'Muhurthachintamani' and 'Shatpanchashika'.

Sun governs 'I am' ness (aham) in humans. Moon governs the mind. Jupiter is responsible for the wisdom. Saturn shapes the experiences. Mars dictates the courage in persons. Mercury controls the intellect. Venus influences the love life. Uranus and Neptune have an effect at a different level. Pluto does not influence the individual much.

Twenty seven stars in the path of the ecliptic (path around the sun) are identified. They are divided into 12 groups or 'rasis'. These rasis are further identified into three subgroups depending upon the nature of their performance.

Dynamic	Inert	Poise
Aries	Taurus	Gemini
Cancer	Leo	Virgo
Libra	Scorpio	Sagittarius
Capricorn	Aquarius	Pisces

It is beyond the scope of this book to discuss further about the planets, stars and rasis or zodiac signs.

CHAPTER 10

Upavedas

There are also four subvedic scriptures or Upa-Vedas. They are briefly explained:

1. Ayurveda:

It deals with the health and welfare of mankind. Ayurveda has been mentioned in Rigveda. This indicates that this science is in practice even 6000 years ago. Ayu means life or lifespan. The knowledge that pertains to maintenance of healthy life and providing ways and means of overcoming physical and mental disorders is the subject matter of Ayurveda. This science is meant for worldly life and life beyond it. This sastra was revealed to sage Bharadwaja by the Almighty. It recognizes 'Panchamahabhuta' the five basic elements with which the world is composed, namely, ether, air, fire, water and earth. Prana is the primary source that sustains life in living beings. The influence of Vata (air), Pitta (fire) and Kapha (water and earth) on prana is the governing principle of Ayurveda. Satwa, Rajas and Tamas are responsible for the whole creation. Out of tamas matter is born. Out of rajas mind and sensory organs function. From satwa intelligence and understanding are born. These forces act in the body. One force causes precipitation of matter (construction of tissues etc.). Another force causes combustion – destruction and decomposition of material tissues and cells to work out the functions of the body or in other words produces calories. A balance between the two forces is produced by a third pulsating force. This produces 'Peristalysis' of the matter in the body. Pulsation is called 'vata'. Materialization is called 'sleshma'. Combustion is called 'pitta'. Atreya Samhita dated 4000-3000 B.C. is the oldest treatise on Ayurveda. It is considered as an adjunct to Atharvanaveda (upaveda). All healing methods such as yoga, aroma, meditation, gems, diet, colour, herbs, and even jyotish in addition to surgery are considered for treatment in Ayurveda. Ayurveda classifies general diseases into six categories.

- those caused by wind,
- those caused by bile,
- those caused by mucus,

- those caused by combination of the above three,
- those caused by infection (virus) and
- those caused by curse.

Ayurvedic medicines are also classified into five categories:

- those that are derived from herbs,
- those that are derived from minerals,
- those that are derived from animals,
- auto vaccine and
- mantras and their applications.

It is believed that several otherwise incurable diseases can be cured by Ayurveda. Around 1500 B.C. Ayurveda was divided into two main branches: school of physicians and school of surgeons.

The school of physicians: This is based on the teachings of Atreyamaharshi. It is further expanded and codified further by Charaka during early period of 1000 B.C. It contains 8400 metered verses.

The school of surgeons: This is based on Susruta Samhita a treatise on surgery and related information by Susruta. Susruta was the first person in this world who performed plastic surgery. He identified several branches in Ayurveda. They are Kayachikitsa, Shalyatantra, Agadatantra, Shalkyatantra, Bhutavidya, Kumarbhritya, Stritantra, Vajikarana and others which correspond to modern medicine specializations such as, internal medicine, surgery, ophthalmology, psychiatry, paediatrics, gynaecology, science of rejuvenation. Further, 'Rog Nidan' explained pathology. 'Kriyasareera' detailed physiology and 'Rachina Sareera' anatomy. Bhaishajya kalpana dealt with pharmaceuticals.

Ayurveda has also astronomical and astrological connection. It considers that diseases can be due to the influence of malicious planets on human life. This influence can be effectively neutralized. For example, disorders connected with blood and circulatory system, digestion related and physical debility problems are attributed to the negative influence of the planet Sun. Mind related problems, respiratory troubles, coughs and cold are considered to be due to the adverse influence of the planet Moon. In this way all the planets are associated with various diseases and disorders. Certain plants and creepers are recommended for neutralizing these negative effects. The suggested herbal plants grow under the direct influence of these planets.

Amalaka plant is suggested for the disease caused by the planets Venus, Mercury and Moon. Aswagandha is good for Ketu and Mercury planets.

Bilva is good for Sun and Mercury and Makaradhwaja is found to be excellent for combating the negative effects of all the nine planets

Around 500 A.D. Vagbhatta compiled a third treatise on Ayurveda in corporating the teachings of both Charaka and Susruta titled Astanga Hridaya. The famous Buddhist Mahayana monk Nagarjuna wrote a commentary on Susruta Samhita.

2. Dhanurveda

It explains the art of archery and the science of war-fare,

Dhanurveda was revealed to sage Viswamitra by Lord Brahma and Lord Shiva. Agnipurana contains the earliest extant manual on Dhanurveda. Patanjali's Yogasutras explained (3 century B.C.) the technique of meditating single mindedly on points located inside the body. This information was used later in martial arts. The various mudra finger movements taught by Yogachara of Buddhism are also adapted to martial arts. Indian martial arts became systematic only durng first millennium A.D. according to historians. The knowledge possessed by the great archers of Itihasas Rama, Parasurama, Arjuna and the great teachers Drona and others is not available through any of the existing scriptures. The 'astras' used by them were invoked by chanting mantras (energy fields of vibrations). During Gupta period (240-480 A.D.) weapons belonging to 130 different classes were used as per records. Eigth century book Kuvalayamala authored by Udyotana Suri mentioned that even Brahmin youth from all over the subcontinent were learning martial arts in established schools of those times.

3. Gandharvaveda

It is concerned with music and musical scales. The universe is created from vibrations. The sound produced by different frequencies of vibrations creates the eternal music of nature. These fundamental frequencies of vibrations and the rhythm of nature which creates balance and harmony between nature and the creation is reflected by the ancient sages of India in Gandharvaveda. It has been already mentioned that Samaveda is sung according to meters invoking the universal Spirits. The musical melodies are called 'ragas'. Every level of creation is a frequency. For every frequency there is a sound. According to the changing qualities of nature over a day of 24 hours, each day is divided into eight, three hour parts and certain ragas are identified to be appropriate for singing during those periods of the day. For example rag Bhairavi is considered to enliven the energy at sunrise while rag Kedara is deemed to be apt as an evening melody for upliftment of heart and create peace and tranquility.

Music increases brainwave coherence, balances physiology, results in better health and more integrated behaviour in a person. It is claimed that ragas have profound effect on the functioning of the various energy centres in human body called 'chakras' or moods in the path of Kundalini (explained later). Bharata has written a book on Natya Sastra, the first treatise on drama, dance and music. Indian classical music is monophonic in nature and based around a fixed melody called 'raga' played over a fixed drone. The melody is systematically followed on a tala. Indian classical music is of two types, Hindustani and Carnatic There is significant influence of Persian and Arabic music on Hindustani music. The ragas are slow elaborations called 'Alap'. Carnatic music ragas are relatively faster in tempo. The musical sounds are - Sa, Re, Ga, Ma, Pa , Dha, Ni, Sa corresponding to the western sounds - Do, Re, Mi, Fa, So ,La, Ti, Do.

4. Sthapthyaveda

It contains all the learning technology about sculpture. But, in broad reality it can be treated as Indian Architecture. The earliest architectural findings belong to Indus Valley Civilization. The various procedures laid out were developed during late vedic period, Mourya and Gupta periods. Panini's Ashtadhyayi (5th century) mentions about the various images that were worshipped in Hindu temples. The temple is considered as a representation of both the macrocosm (the universe) and the microcosm (the inner space). Initially the construction of vedic altars was considered at length. This knowledge became the precursor to building temples. The concept of Mandala is metaphysical in nature. It is a site plan in architecture. Every site can be divided into grids or modules called 'padas'. Every site is surrounded by eight divine forces or energies. These can be treated as deities. In the east it is the Sun and in the west it is the Varuna or Uranus. In the north it is Kubera the god for wealth and in the south Yama the destroyer of life. The most sacred corner north-east is presided over by Lord Shiva and south east by Agni the fire god. The south-west is controlled by Pitrus or ancestors and north-west is commanded by Vayu the wind god. At the center of the site resides Brahma, the god of creation.

Zoning of the site and disposition of the function is arrived at in a building depending on the position of the god occupying the module or pada . There are several vital and vulnerable energy points where there should be no construction. In case of temples every temple must have a 'Girbha Griha', an inner chamber with space for circumambulation a congregation hall, an optional antechamber and a porch at the front. The Sanctum is coverd at the top by a tower like structure called 'Shikhara'. There are two types of Shikhara constructions. Most of the North Indian temples follow Nagara style, where the tower is bee-hive shaped. In the Dravidian style follwed by temples in the South the shikhara tapers progressively upwards with smaller storeys of pavilions. There are also temples that combine both the styles. The temple plan is a square divided into 64 or 81 smaller squares. The mandalas or divisions are titled Pitha (tripada), Mahapitha (chatushpada), Upapitha (panchapada), Ugrapitha (shashtapada), Manduka or Chandita (ashtapada), and Paramasaayika mandala(navapada). In every building constructed for worship or living Purusha (energy, soul, cosmicman) lives in it. For worship it is again either Sakala or Nishkala worship. Sakala is used for temples where gods with form (murthy) are installed and worshipped. In nishkala style there is no diety installed but the amorphous central place is a great source of power and energy. Commercial buildings use only odd number of modules.

CHAPTER 11

Shatdarsanas

While Upanishads dealt with philosophy or metaphysics and vedantic matters six more disciplines in philosophy emerged. These schools of philosophy based on Vedas are meant for scholars and intellgensia. They are called 'shat-darshanas' These are six different ways of looking at the same Absolute Truth.

(i) The Nyaya System

The **Nyaya** system due to Aksapada Gautama sage (ca 2. century B.C,) deals with the logic of transcending the domain of mind. It is concerned with the mental processes of learning. There are 528 (537, with later additions) sutras or aphorisms contained in 5 chapters. The aim of the nyaya sutras is the attainment of liberation. One must acquire the knowledge of the truth. Knowledge of the truth eliminates miseries, birth cycles, mundane existence, mistakes, false knowledge and thus brings salvation or 'moksha' – freedom of the soul. Gautama says that knowledge of sixteen categories leads to 'moksha'. These 16 are connected with the process of reasoning and the laws of the thought. The nyaya system teaches us the method of investigation.

They are now enumerated.

1. Means of valid knowledge (Pramana): They are the means or instruments by which the right measure (praman) of any object is obtained These are the different processes through which the mind arrives at true knowledge.
2. Objects of valid knowledge (Prameya): All the objects or subjects of right knowledge are prameya. They are 12 in number.
   - Soul (Atma)
   - Body (Sareer)
   - Organs of senses (Indryas)
   - Objects of senses (Arth)
   - Intellect (Budhi)
   - Mind (Manas)

- Activity (Pravritti)
- Faults (Dosh)
- Transmigration (Praityabhav)
- Consequences (Phal)
- Pain (Dukh)
- Emancipation (Apvarg)

3. *Doubt (Samsaya):* This and the remaining 13 are not strictly categories. They are stages through which any logical controversy must pass. While discussing a topic a doubt may arise.
4. *Purpose (Prayojan):* The development of a doubt leads to a basic question as to the motive or reason for discussing the subject. That is prayojan.
5. *Example (Drishtanta):* The discussion should then include several examples to support the argument.
6. *Conclusion (Sidhanta):* With the above an established conclusion could be arrived at.
7. *The costituents of a syllogism *(Avayava):* The arguments of the object are split up. (*A form of reasoning in which a conclusion is drawn from two propositions.)

   Ex: The cow is an animal.

   Because it has four legs.

   All animals have four legs

   A cow has four legs.

   So, a cow is an animal).
8. *Argumentation (Tark):* Refutation of the objection
9. *Ascertainment (Nirnaya):* This is coming to conclusion. In nyaya philosophy these measures are considered not sufficient to settle the question. It proposes that every side of the question must be examined. All the objections must be raised.
10. *Debate (Vada):* A debate must be conducted for this.
11. *Disputations (Jalpa):* There could be all sorts of wrangling.
12. *Destructive criticism (Vitanda):* This is to utilize all sorts of arguments to get a point through the debate.
13. *Fallacy (Hetvabhasa):* Use of fallacies in reasoning for the sake of an argument.

14. *Quibble (Chala):* Just raising objections and trying to be evasive on issues.
15. Refutations (Jati): Giving futile replies.
16. Defeat of the opponent's points (Nigrahsthan): Putting an end to all discussions by a demonstration of the opponets incapacity for argument.

Valid knowledge can be obtained by four means. They are :

- Perception (Pratyaksha)
- Inference (Anumana)
- Comparison (Upamana) and
- Verbal testimony (Shabd)

Invalid knowledge is information that involves memory, doubt, error and hypothetical arguments.

Nyaya develops the theory of causation. According to it cause and effect should be homogenous in nature. It defines a cause as an unconditioned and invariable antecedent of an effect. The effect is a new beginning and is not already contained in the cause. That is to say that the effect does not preexist in the cause. Thus, it is at variance with Sankhya and Vedantist views. As has been already explained Nyaya, aphorisms support a five part syllogism. (A syllogism is a form of reasoning in which conclusion is drawn from two propositions).

Three kinds of causes are identified. They are:

(i) Inherent or material cause. (the substance out of which an effect is produced).

(ii) Noninherent cause (which helps in the production of the cause) and

(iii) Efficient cause (the power that helps the material cause produce the effect).

God is not the material cause of the universe since atoms and souls are also eternal. He is the efficient cause. The aim of every philosophy must be to give an analytical demonstration of the universe. The nyaya doctrine only mentions objects or subjects to be known. Vaiseshika science developed by Kanada analysed the things and laid down the principles that lead to final understanding of things, called liberation.

(ii) The Vaiseshika System

The Vaiseshika system proposed by Kanada is famous for its description of atomic structure of the universe. It deals with the knowledge of the existing things like Dravya (physical matter), Guna (mental characteristics) such as satva, rajas and tamas as well as karma (works). Vaiseshika is metaphysical in nature which incorporates logic. It has 373 sutras or aphorisms organized into 12 chapters. Kanada lived at Prabhas Kshetra near Dwaraka in Gujarat state around 600 B.C.

The word Visesha means particularity pointed out by differences in characteristics. All objects of experience called padartha are classified into six categories. They are:

1. Dravya – Substance,
2. Guna – Property or Quality,
3. Karma – Action,
4. Samanya – Genarality of properties, which can not be perceived but can be inferred and is the relation between the cause and effect,
5. Visesha – Particularity and
6. Samavaya – Co-inherence or perpetual intimate relation.

A seventh category was added later called Abhava or non existence. The first three of them namely, substance, quality and action have real objective existence. The later three, generality, particularity and inherence are of logical type. They are the outcomes of intellectual discrimination.

Dravya or substances are of nine types. The first five are the elements or 'bhutas' earth, water, fire, air and ether. The other four are kal or time, dik or space, atma or soul, and manas or mind. The first four and the last are atomic in nature. Also the first four are eternal in their ultimate atom. They are also noneternal in their various compounds. Mind is eternal. It does not pervade everywhere, like soul. It is atomic. It can admit only one thought at a time.

The nine substances possess 17 basic qualities. They are :

colour (rupa), taste (rasa), smell or odour (gandha), touch (sparsa), numbers (sankhya), measure or size (parimana), separateness or individuality (prithaktvam), conjunction (samyoga), disconjunction (vibhaga), priority (paratva), posterity (aparatva), intellect or understanding (buddhi), pleasure (sukh), pain (dukh), desire (icha), aversion (dvesha) and volition (prayatna).

Prasastapada added seven more later and they are gravity (gurutva), fluidity (dravyatva), viscosity (snaih), faculty (samskar), merit (dharma), demerit (adharma), and sound (shabd). Of these volition, desire, aversion, pleasure, pain, merit and demerit are the properties of the soul. The rest 16 belong to material substances.

The third category action or karma is of five types.

1. Elevation or going upwards (Utkshepana).
2. Depression or going downwards (Arakshepana).
3. Contraction (Akunchan).
4. Expansion or dilation (Sanprasaran).
5. Motion (Gaman).

Samanya, the fourth category of padarthas deals with the generality of properties which are twofold.They are:

(a) Higher and lower generality,
(b) Genus and species. Further,
(c) Samanya is that which makes many things into one.

The fifth category visesha or particularity belongs to nine eternal substances of category. All of them have an eternal ultimate difference. This difference distinguishes each from the others. In fact, it is from this point that this science of investigation derived its name as vaiseshika. Visesha is responsible for decrease in the number of the constituent parts.

The sixth category samavaya or coherence is of only one kind. It is the coinherence between the substance and its qualities, between a genus and its individuals, between any object and the general idea connected with it. It is thought to be a real entity. It can be seen as the relation between the cause and the effect. (Ex: container and the contained).

Knowledge of the padartha helps in understanding nature of this world. By knowing the similarities and differences of substances which constitute their dharma, the ultimate Reality can be grasped.

Kanada believed that the world was the result of a coincidence of the unforeseen force of actions. He considered that the primal activities of atoms and souls to be responsible for this coincidence (adrishta). The followers of Kanada later introduced god as the efficient cause of the world. The atoms are considered as the material cause of the world.

The unthinking atoms do not possess the power and intelligence to run the universe. The actions of the atoms must be governed by an Omniscient and Omnipotent Divine force. Scriptures and logical conclusions compel us to admit the existence of Divinity. The intelligence that creates the coincidence is called God. The five basic elements are the effect of that intelligence. That is God.

Atomic theory: The world is made up of atoms, which are countless and eternal. They are aggregated and disintegrated repeatedly by the power of the coincidence. An atom is eternal and has no cause for its existence. Atom is smaller than the smallest, invisible, imperceptible and intangible to our sense. Each atom has its own particularity or visesha. They combine first into an aggragate of two called Dvyanu. Three of them combine into an aggregate called Trasarenu.This is called peeluvaaka vaada or chemical theory. Peelu means an atom or paramanu. Things differ due to difference in chemical composition.

There are four classes of paramanus. They are paramanus of earth, water, fire and air. Individual atoms are engaged in combination and disintegration after some time. The vaiseshika cosmogony is dualistic as it admits the existence of eternal atoms and eternal souls simultaneously. The body is subtle in dissolution and gross in creation. The time, place, family and circumstances of birth and the life span are determined by the so called coincidence. The individual souls are many, eternal and separate from one another. They are distinct from body, mind and senses. But, the soul experiences desire, aversion, pleasure, pain, volition, merit, demerit. They are infinite and omnipresent. They diffuse everywhere throughout the universe. The soul and mind are not objects of perception. In the state of salvation or moksha the soul gets disconnected from all and regains its independence.

Birth is the result of conjunction of soul with body, sense and life caused by right and wrong conduct and the disjunction is called death. Liberation is the disconnection of the soul with the body, while simultaneously no potential body exists for rebirth. Conjunction of soul, with mind and object produces pleasure and pain. Experiencing pleasure leads to desire to have more pleasure. This pleasure is caused by objects. Various objects of pleasure are desired successively. If pain results from objects then aversion is produced.

Desire, aversion and infatuation (raga, dvesha and moha) are the defects (doshas) that bind the doer to this world. These defects incite activity and hence attachment results leading to rebirth. When the attachment is overcome by true knowledge the defects are removed, activity disappears and liberation occurs.

Kanada has failed to explain how the initial activity was imparted to atoms. Also the successive evolution of life in plants, animals and humans, creation of living matter from nonliving matter were also not explained. If 'Atma' were to be padartha, then it will have growth and decay. It will be bound to the results of actions. Atma becomes a householder. This is against Vedas.

(iii) The Sankhya System

The Sankhya system presented by rishi Kapila explains the harmonious interrelationship of numbers to nature and spirit. Sankhya means enumeration or analysis of universe. Some western commentators called sankhya philosophy as synthetic enumeration and numeral philosophy. It considers the world as real, balanced, intelligent activity and matter. It exhorts one to understand the difference between nature (prakriti) and man (purusha). There are six chapters which recommend humans to obtain freedom from the three kinds of miseries that afflict them. Sankhya assumes that the world is full of miseries. These are

1. *Adhyatmic:* due to one self,
2. *Adhibhoutic:* due to elements of nature and
3. *Adhidaivic:* due to supernatural causes.

Matter is eternal and coexistent with spirit. Together they create the world. Twenty four categories of existence are presented by Kapila. Some are of the opinion that he collecetd the scattered thoughts of Hindu philosophy from various upanishads and gave a systematic shape to them. Though one may not agree with some of the propositions at this stage of evolution, yet, the work is of great value in terms of philosophic analysis.

The Universal Soul, is called 'Paramatma' or 'Purusha'. The manifest energy of purusha is Prakriti. At the instance of Purusha, Prakriti acts and Purusha thus provoked assumes different Jeeva forms.

All objects fall under two categories. Purusha is spirit or consciousness. Prakriti is matter. Purusha is the non attributive transcendental self which is pure consciousness that is independent, free and unknowable. Purusha is neither produced nor does it produce. Prakriti is composed of three qualities or gunas called satva (goodness or balanced nature), rajas (passion, energy, or activity) and tamas (inactivity, grossness or darkness). Initially they are in balance or equipoise. The whole world comes out when the balance is disturbed.

1. Prakriti: All physical events are considered the manifestation of evolution of prakriti. This is the original primordial thing or eternall existing essence which produces everything. It is the most subtle potentiality that is behind every thing that is created.
2. It produces 'mahat' first. It is held responsible for 'buddhi' or intellect.
3. From it 'selfconsciousness' or 'ego' (aham) is produced. It is responsible for the feeling of I'ness in beings.
4. From aham the five subtle elements (tanmatras) sound (shabd),
5. form (rupa),
6. touch or tangibility (sparsa),
7. taste (rasa), and.
8. smell (gandha) the subtle form of the great five elements are produced. Each of the tanmatras contain all the three gunas or qualities.
9. Manas or antahkarana is evolved from the totality of sattva aspect of aham.

   In addition, two sets of organs (indriyas), both external and internal, are produced. They are:
10. the two hands,
11. the two legs,
12. the vocal apparatus,
13. the urino-genital organs and
14. the anus which are called karmendriyas or organs of action . They contain the rajasic aspect of the aham.

Jnanendriyas which are the sense organs are also five in number and they are

15. the two eyes,
16. the two ears,
17. the nose,
18. the tongue and
19. the skin. They represent the sattvic aspect of aham.

Further the five gross elements that are evolved are :

20. earth,
21. water,
22. fire
23. air and
24. ether. They represent the tamasic aspect of aham.

Purusha is the twentyfifth outcome

Each sentient being is a purusha. He is limitless and exists beyond the physical body. When purusha gets confused and considers himself as the physical body bondage (samsara) occurs. Loss of discriminative knowledge is responsible for it. Once purusha becomes aware of the difference between the conscious self and the unconscious prakriti, the illusion is removed and liberation takes place.

The existence of god can not be proved. Hence, He can not exist. Unchanging Eswara can not be the cause for a changing world as the effect. Later the followers of Sankhya incorporated the existence of God in their philosophy.

It follows 'prakriti parinama vaada'. The effect preexists in the cause. Cause and effect are different forms of the same thing with time displacement. The effect is imbedded within the cause inherently. It is only a transformation of the cause. The cause is primal nature. The evolution begins with primordial matter. Thus, nature gets transformed into multiple objects. Every evolution is followed by a dissolution when all the physical objects merge into nature. This is the primordial matter. According to sankhya philosophy prakriti is pure potentiality and it evolves itself into the 24 qualities enumerated earlier. Now a few quotes from the aphorisms will be presented.

"Sanhat prardhatvat": Things that combine and lose their identity reappear in another form.

"Trigun adivipryat": This is so since soul contains the three gunas satva (passivity), rajas (activity) and tamas (grossness).

"Adhishthach": That soul can not be material since it has control over the unintelligent prakriti.

"Bhoktribhavat": It can not be material since it is the experience.

Thus, it is emphasized that soul is a separate entity different from nature. The question pertaining to the characteristic of soul is further clarified:

'Jadprakasha yogat prakas': Soul is essentially light. Intelligence is an attribute of the soul but, soul has no quality (Nirgunam, Nirvisesham). Sankhya system believes in Vedas. However, the system contends that the soul mentioned in Vedas is the genus of the multiple souls of Sankhya system.

Soul is not bound to matter. Liberation is also an illusion. Soul is always free and does not experience any pleasure or pain. Prakriti created universe for the release of soul and for its own release.

This is how the sankhya system is explained.

(iv) The Yoga System

The word yoga is the term derived from the root 'Yuj' which means union. Literally yoga is the term used for the process that enables the individuals charactrerized by 'Self' unite himself with the Universal Self or Cosmic Mind. Stated differently it refers to the process that leads to merging of jeevatma with Paramatma. Lord Krishna explained Sankhya, Jnana, Karma and Bhakti yoga methods in Gita of Mahabharata. Scriptures explained 33 methods for this achievement. These yoga methods are – Abhava, Adhyatma, Anna, Asparsa, Abhyasa, Agni, Ashtanga, Bhava, Bhakti, Dhyana, Kriya, Lambika, Laya, Maha, Mantra, Hatha, Hamsa, Nada, Pashupata, Raja, Karma, Sankhya, Sanyasi, Samputa, Kundalini, Samarambha, Saptanga, Shadanga, Shiva, Sparsa, Sachanda, Taraka and Vahni yogas. The books that explained the methods of yoga are :-

Yoga vashishta, Patanjali's yoga aphorisms of second century, Eswarakrishna Sankhya karika and Yogakara by Asanga of fourth century, Yogakundalini Upanishad and Yoga Chntamani by Shivananda Saraswati and Yogakarnika by Aghorananda of eighteenth century and Yoga karnika by Vachaspati and others. Shri Aravinda yogi explained an integral system of yoga. While Yoga Vashishta contains the philosophy of life explained by sage Vasishta to Lord Rama, the explanation for living a life was given to Arjuna in Bhagavadgita by Lord Krishna at the beginning of the great war at Kurukshetra. Eventhough the latter is more popular, the science of yoga explained by Sage Patanjali has acquired wider recognition. This is enumerated in the following, and it explains Raja-yoga or Ashtanga yoga for achieving unity of body and mind leading to supreme bliss.

There are four parts or padas in this Yoga sastra. They are called Samadhi pada, Sadhana pada, Vibhuti pada and Kaivalya pada.

Samadhi Pada :

In this first part there are 51 sutras (Aphorisms). They are stated as

1. Now yoga will be explained.
2. Yoga is steadying the reflexive mind (chitta) from indulging into various thoughts (vrittis). Vrittis are those thoughts from the external world that influence the mind, thoughts and actions.
3. When this is practiced focusing on the inner self will be achieved. The seer (purusha) enters his unmodified state.
4. Otherwise one moves with his own modifications.
5. There are five modifications which may be problematic or nonproblematic.
6. They are right knowledge, indiscrimination or wrong understanding of right Reference, verbal delusion, sleep and rememberance.
7. Right knowledge is of three types – personal witnessing, inference, reliable evidence or proof.
8. indiscrimination comes when things are understood in the wrong way without considering the real nature of them.
9. Verbal delusion is due to jumping to conclusions fast without proper understanding.
10. During sleep mind experiences voidness.
11. Impressions retained in the mind due to past experience stay in memory as smriti.
12. Through practice and nonattachment the effect of vrittis on mind can be controlled.
13. Practice is the continuous effort put to subdue the vrittis from influencing the mind (chitta).
14. This effort must be continuous for a long time while simultaneously good deeds must be performed. Then one can obtain a hold on the mind.
15. Nonsubmission to those desires that attract sense organs through sight and hearing is called detachment.
16. Keeping attention on the higher self, giving up the three gunas (sathva, rajas, tamas), is called higher nonattachment or renunciation (para vairagya).

17. Wakefulness (conscious process) and unconsciousness are called 'prajnata' and 'ajnata' states. In 'samprajnata' state a person falsely feels that he has attained detachment. Supraconscious or 'asamprajnata' state, a condition where unification of the self with the Divine occurs in perfect consciousness is the real detachment. Samprajnata Samadhi may endow some powers.
18. Beyond the state of asamprajnata lies a state of absolute unification with mind completely ceasing all the activities. Chitta contains only unmanifested impressions.
19. Death with attachments retained, leads to another birth carrying the attachments forward.
20. With faith understanding the Truth, and remembering the objective some attain the state of Samadhi.
21. Some attain Samadhi with utter dedication without any distraction.
22. The occurrence of samadhi state depends on the modes of practice, namely, gentle, forceful and a middle path.
23. By total surrender to God also, Samadhi state is attainable.
24. Iswara is unaffected by miseries, attachments, fruits of action and is untouched by even thoughts about them.
25. He is all knowing Infinite whom no one can surpass (being only a part of him).
26. As Iswar is not limited by time He is the teacher to the ancients also.
27. Pranava AUM is His sound. His manifesting word is AUM.
28. The way to understand Him is to meditate on AUM.
29. By that, realization of God in everything happens without any obstacle.
30. The obstacles are sickness, carelessness, doubt, committing errors, laziness, feeling restless, experiencing illusions as yogic experiences, and inability to concentrate and stabilize the mind. They are all vrittis of chitta.
31. Sadness, depression, unintended movements of body and its organs and irregular breathing are similar obstacles.
32. To overcome these obstacles continuous practice of one subject (AUM) is required.

33. Friendship with happy people, compassion people stricken by grief, happiness towards good people and ignoring bad people are to be practiced.
34. In taming chitta, the reflesive mind breath control is helpful.
35. Chitta can be also controlled by contemplating on the mind and its distracting influences.
36. Realizing that the Self is happiness and meditating on that light is also helpful.
37. By meditating on those people who have given up all attachments.
38. By contemplating on the process of dreaming and sleeping chitta can be controlled.
39. By meditating on anything that appeals as good.
40. By meditating on anything from atom to Infinite, mind can be tamed.
41. After, all the vrittis of mind disappear, the pure and the absolute remains. The mind only reflects things as pure crystal, but does not get attached to them.
42. Experiencing sound, knowing its meaning, and the knowledge about it results in duality of subject and object.
43. Once the vrittis are completely annihilated then the real self glows with light. There will be no more doubts (nirvitarka). This state is called samadhi.
44. The change occurs not only in the things physically seen, but also in mental attitude. Even finer aspects get influenced.
45. With the exception of the soul, all the finer aspects, namely, the three qualities, the five attributes of senses and the components of mind will be realized.
46. This is 'sabeeja samadhi' or samadhi state with seed.
47. Once the illusory nature of experience is annihilated, the pure Self is experienced.
48. The consciousness in that state is Truth or 'Satya'.
49. The knowledge experienced then will be unique.
50. The impression then created will destroy all other impressions.

51. In this state of consciousness called 'Ritumbhara' the Self alone glows Seedless or 'Nirbeeja Samadhi' is attained.

This is the **Samadhi pada** or the **first quartet** of Patanjali's Science of Yoga.

Sadhana pada

The second pada or second quartet is called sadhana pada. It contains 55 sutras.

1. Mortification, self study, and complete surrender to Almighty (the fruits of action) constitute 'Kriya yoga'.
2. Observance of kriya yoga in daily life leads to experiencing samadhi. All the obstacles in the way will be removed.
3. The grief giving obstructions are five, namely, ignorance (avidya), I am' ness (asmita), attachment (raga) antipathy (dvesha) and dogmatism (abhinivesh).
4. Ignorance is the main cause for all other obstructions which may be dormant, weakened, dispersing and reappearing and strengthening.
5. Ignorance is considering impermanent as permanent, unclean as clean, grief as happiness and nonself as self.
6. I am' ness is understanding that the seer and the power behind the sight are one and the same (egoism).
7. Desire to be happy is attachment.
8. Fear of unhappiness is aversion.
9. Like the ignorant, even the learned possess dogmatism due to their own nature.
10. 'Klesha', the grief giving obstructions, also called 'samskaras' are very fine. They do not get removed very easily. For this 'chitta' the reflective mind which is the effect must be resolved into its cause 'egoism'.
11. To get rid of the waves of thoughts that influence the mind worship of god is the only way.
12. The obstructions that appear are due to actions committed previously knowingly or unknowingly and they remain as impressions in the mind. From whence, the cycle of births and deaths follows.

13. So long these impressions of the past exist, birth, life and experiences, the fruits of actions remain.
14. These actions give pleasure or pain depending upon the nature of the actions, good or bad.
15. To a discriminating person everything brings pain only. They may be due to some consequences or cravings for happiness due to one's own false impression of thoughts and due to the three qualities (gunas).
16. The grief that may materialize in future (agami) can be escaped by taking care of the present and future actions.
17. The misery arises due to the union of the seer and the seen which remain unclear.
18. The whole nature that is composed of the three gunas , five elements and the five senses is for both experience and for liberation.
19. The three gunas have four states, namely, recognized, unrecognized, ingrained with features for recognition and nonexistence of such features.
20. The seer within the body is pure. While viewing through the mind the seer looks through the layers of the intellect.
21. The benefit of the sight is for the seer only.
22. For a yogi the world disappears, but, for the others it remains.
23. The soul, the mind and the seen world in view of their interrelations create experiences.
24. Ignorance is its cause.
25. Once ignorance is banished these interrelations disappear. Then, only the seer remains.
26. Once this knowledge is attained enlightenment results and bondages are broken.
27. The light in that stage is realized in seven steps. (physical, vital, mental, and knowledge planes, group consciousness, 'paranirvana' or 'Brahmalok' (the realm of the Absolute) and 'mahaparanirvana' or Absolute consciousness.
28. Once yoga is practiced and implemented, all the impurities leave. Knowledge becomes effulgent till self realisation is achieved.

29. Yama, Niyama, Asana, Pranayama, Pratyahara, Dharana, Dhyana and Samadhi are the eight organs of yoga.
30. Non-violence (ahimsa), truthfulness (satya), non-stealing (asteya), continence (brahmacharya), and non-receiving (aparigraha) are called Yama.
31. Yoga is to be practiced forever and is not limited by time, place and nationality.
32. Purity of body and mind (shaucha), happiness (santosha), mortification (tapas), self study (swadhyaya), and surrender to God (Iswarpranidhan) constitute Niyama.
33. Distracting thoughts in practicing yoga are to countered by thoughts of opposing nature.
34. Violent and stealing nature, anger and desire are inimical to yoga whether committed, caused or approved. Such qualities cause immense pain. These undesirable qualities are to be destroyed through positive feelings that counter them.
35. In the presence of one who achieved perfect control on violence, all will behave with him in a friendly manner.
36. By establishing truthfulness in behaviour one will experience the fruits of that immediately.
37. He, who never steals gets all the riches.
38. Through establishing continence one gains strength and capability.
39. When one does not wish to receive any thing, he gets the knowledge of the past births.
40. One, who practices cleanliness loses attachment to body; neither does he gets attached to other bodies.
41. Practicing of cleanliness enables one to experience balance of mind, make him eligible for concentration and fit for control of senses and organs leading to self realization.
42. Staying thus in a state of contentment he gets still higher happiness.
43. Through mortification and due to the removal of physical and mental impurities the body and senses attain full energization.
44. Continuous practice of studying vedic literature leads to connection with the personal deity.
45. Complete surrender to God enables realization of the state of samadhi.

46. Posture (asana) is that which is stable and pleasant.
47. By dedicating mind to the Infinite Absolute Reality, effortlessly posture can be achieved with effort.
48. By that, dualities do not affect or obstruct.
49. Attainment of posture leads to stillness in respiration.
50. When this happens, all internal and external efforts cease. Place, time and observation attain their natural disposition. Breath appears fine and subtle. Time appears as either short or long.
51. A new state of existence beyond internal and external manifests.
52. The light of the Self expands unlimited.
53. Mind becomes eligible for Dharana or concentration.
54. Withdrawal of senses leads chitta (mind) to stay in its true state.
55. In this state the senses are completely under control.

Thus ends the Sadhana pada.The third part is called Vibhuti pada and contains 56 sutras

Vibhuti pada

1. Holding the mind on any assigned thing is called ‘ Dharana.’ (concentration)
2. Unification of the mind with the object of dharana in complete exclusion of everything else is called ‘Dhyana’ (meditation)
3. When the mind reflects only on the meaning of the meditated object, giving up its name, form, nature and others, the state is called ‘Samadhi’.
4. Simultaneous holding of dharana, dhyana and samadhi is called ‘Samyama’.
5. The light of knowledge will be the result when that is achieved.
6. This light of knowledge should be able to utilized in diverse fields by the practitioner.
7. Out of the eight organs of yoga, these three are more of internal nature than the five that preceded.

8. In seedless state (Nirbeeja Samadhi), even these three are external.
9. The disturbing impressions should be countered by always controlling impressions.

   Then all impressions will become controlling modifications.
10. Continuous control of the impressions of the mind leads to peaceful flow of thoughts.
11. Slowly, the disturbing waves of thoughts from the mind will cease to manifest and Samadhi is achieved.
12. Since the impressions of the past and the impressions of the present have the same features single pointedness of the mind (chitta) is achieved.
13. Due to this, the body form, senses and their functions experience a change.
14. That which is inherent in all actions of control, in them that reemerges and in uncontrollable fine aspects is called 'Dharmi', the qualified. (Yogi understands everything.)
15. According to the stage of evolution the changes occur.
16. By observing these changes with samyama it is possible to know the past and the future (seer, seen, seeing the triputi; unites.)
17. Application of samyama on the word spoken, on the meaning of it and the knowledge from it pertaining to all beings leads to understanding of all sounds.
18. By the application of samyama on the past impressions, knowledge of past birth is obtained.
19. By applying samyama to other's mind, their thoughts will be known.
20. The knowledge is limited to their thoughts only, and not about the objects of the thoughts.
21. By applying samyama on the body and its form, the power of others to grasp the body form through eyes will be frozen. (The yogi will not be seen by others).
22. By this, the principle of disappearance of sound, touch, taste, and smell is explained.
23. Two types of results of past actions (karma) exist. One that fructifies immediately and one that bears fruit gradually and is experienced later. By applying samyama on all actions

knowledge of existence and dissolution of the worlds will be known. All portents will be known.

24. By samyama on such qualities as strength, friendship, yogi attains those qualities.
25. With samyama on the strength of elephant, one attains the strength of an elephant.
26. By making samyama on the external world, understanding the subtle, the fine and the remote objects is obtained.
27. By samyama on sun, knowledge of the world is attained.
28. By samyama applied to moon, knowledge of the stars is obtained.
29. By samyama on pole star, the movement of poles is understood.
30. By applying to navel, knowledge of the body constitution is obtained.
31. Applying on the hollow of the throat, hunger is conquered.
32. On the 'kurma nadi' steadiness of the mind is achieved. (One finds the centre of his own circle. Unperturbed state under all conditions)
33. Samyama applied to light visualized in the head, great masters (siddhas) can be seen.
34. On applying to capability everything is understood.
35. By samyama on heart, knowledge of mind is obtained which transcends everything.
36. With the mind fixed on the innerself undisturbed, applying samyama on all external forms that are meant for the self, knowledge of the purusha (Self) is understood.
37. This achieved, subtle and super natural powers (in sense organs) result.
38. Since these powers arise out of impressions, they work as obstacles.
39. By releasing from the bondage of the body, yogi can enter into another body.
40. By conquering 'udana' component of ' prana' yogi is not afflicted by water, mud, thorns and the like and can easily walk over them.

41. By conquering 'samana' component of 'prana' yogi attains effulgence or glorification.
42. By samyama on the relation between hearing and cosmic sound, divine audibility (Divya shravana shakti) is achieved.
43. By samyama on the relation between body and ether, visualizing as the one between cotton wool and the sky, power to fly in the sky is achieved.
44. Even when mind is in contact with the external world, nonexistence of impressions is a state called disembodiedness is attained. By samyama on that state the effulgence of the self gets unbounded.
45. Control over the five elements is obtained by samyama on the gross and fine forms of the elements, their essential characteristics, their interrelationships and their utility.
46. From that comes the attainment of the great eight powers (siddhis) such as miniscule size, very heavy or large body, (anima and garima).
47. The body gets glory, strength, beauty and diamond like luster and hardness.
48. If samyama is applied on the nature of the organs, their specialities, the ego that is working inside them, their expansion and their utility control over the organs is attained.
49. By that body gets the speed of the mind, and even without the need of the physical organs, the sense organs grasp the things. Control over nature that is beyond the qualities is achieved.
50. The distinction between self and purusha (intellect and I'ness) remains nominal. Yogi achieves omniscience and omnipotence.
51. Renunciation of that leads to elimination of seeds of evil. That is 'Kaivalya', the liberation.
52. All overtures in that state to yogi have no effect on him. Otherwise, attachments will reappear.
53. Discrimination comes from samyama on the minutest part of time and its precession.
54. By this knowledge, recognition of life forms in relation to their species, characteristics, places of habitat will become known.
55. Knowledge obtained from this awakening entails liberation. Then everything becomes understood without any effort.

56. When absolute purity is obtained, for both the intellect and the soul, only the self exists. This is called 'kaivalya' or liberation (Self realization).

Kaivalya pada

1. Some attain powers by birth. Some obtain using medicines. Others through prayers (mantras) or by meditation or samadhi.
2. Changes in a nation or in a community occur due to nature. Changes in internal nature cause changes in the personality.
3. All means of yoga assist in removing the obstacles but are not responsible for the changes. Nature only is responsible for samadhi or yogasidhi. This is similar to a farmer's job in the field. But, the crop comes out of the seeds due to nature only.
4. All the thoughts in the mind arise out of the 'self' or 'I'ness' that exists in the finite body.
5. There is an individual mind from which all thoughts emanate. The distinction between different persons arises from this.
6. The mind that is left clean due to meditation in yoga is the one that does not produce fruits of action.That 'chitta' alone is controlled.
7. For a yogi 'chitta' is neither white nor black nor is it made up of a mixture of the both. But this is so in others' case. (there are no fruits of action to yogi).
8. Actions of persons who are not yogis reflect the attitudes pertaining to right conduct, sinful bahaviour and a combination of the both.
9. Eventhough persons are separated by births, by the countries they inhabited in their past lives, by the time between their previous births, still, they carry forward their mental impressions (samskaras) along with their seeds. These prevent change in their attitude.
10. Since atma (soul) is immortal, the desire to live remains forever. In all the births it remains. For all the births that desire forms the basis.
11. Reasons, actions, their fruits, their bases, their places of existence are responsible for carrying over these impressions (vasanas). When they are annihilated the impressions (vrittis) disappear.

12. Only in conceptual form past and future are different from the present. The actions of the past become seeds for the future and work at present as desires that impel actions.
13. These impressions while working either in manifest or subtle form together with the triad of qualities create the illusion that the self is acting.
14. But the transformation is infact caused by that Supreme Reality which is behind all the things.
15. Eventhough all minds have come from one universal mind, the individual minds work differently.
16. The intentions of mind produces many forms. These forms work according to the mind that created them.
17. Based upon the intention of the mind to allow a relationship with an object to exist or not, the knowledge or ignorance about that object is dependent.
18. The lord (Purusha) of the mind is unchanging. He always observes the impressions of the mind. Purusha also observes the underlying reasons that produce the results.
19. Mind is known through its thoughts. It is not self luminous.
20. Mind can not comprehend two things at the same time.
21. There is no possibility that another mind observes the existing mind, in which case there could be several minds in that way.
22. The light from atma illumines external things without getting attached to them. When it reflects on the mind 'self' comes to knowledge.
23. In that state, even if the mind contemplates on several things it converts them as assisting tools and remains in its unified state.
24. Even when uncountable impressions of the past pertaining to happy and /or unhappy moments arise in memory, they are looked upon as separate from the self and staying oneself in the 'self ' results.
25. Then mind stabilizes in the knowledge of the self. Its manifest form will be seen as light.
26. In that state as mind is always pulled towards discriminating intellect, it tends always towards the 'self'.

27. Even in that state I'ness and mine'ness cause interruptions due to mental impressions.
28. In the same way as ignorance is annihilated, these obstacles should also be removed.
29. The desire to experience the light of the self will be also given up by samyama, then the yogi experiences the light of intellect and wisdom. Righteousness will cover him up as Samadhi.
30. Then all actions (karmas) that create unhappiness will disappear.
31. The practitioner overcomes all the layers of ignorance and becomes pure. As knowledge expands ignorance is reduced.
32. The triad of attributes work only to train. Since the job is accomplished, they will lose their influence on yogi.
33. The changes that occur every moment slowly cease to happen. The last transformation remains fixed.
34. Since the four basic desires ('Dharma, Artha, Kama, and Moksha') righteousness, wealth, wants, and liberation are not in the plane of existence, the triad of qualities dissolve into the nature from where they have arisen. Then the self alone remains. This is called pure consciousness (Kaivalya).

    Thus the Kaivalya pada ends. Patanjali's yoga sutra or aphorisms also end here. Patanjali has not only accepted all the formulations of Sankhya doctrine but also accepted a Supreme Spirit or Eeswara. But since this Eeswara is identified as jeevatma the concept goes against Vedas. If jeeva is Eeswara then the heterogeneity in creation can not be explained.

(v) Poorva Mimamsa

Mimamsa in Sanskrit means investigation, inquiry or discussion. It can be said that in this context mimamsa means an investigation into the proper interpretation of vedic texts. Poorva and Uttara are prefixed to indicate that the interpretation pertains to the earlier and later parts of Vedas. Hence the topics poorva mimamsa and uttara mimamsa are chosen as the titles for the two important darsanas, about which a brief introduction follows. Poorva mimamsa is also known as 'dharma' mimamsa as it investigates into dharma (righteousness) established by Vedas. Poorva mimamsa mainly speaks about 'karma' or work schedule to be performed daily to reach the selfhood. Hence it is also called karma mimamsa. It teaches the method of reaching the Supreme Lord in a progressive manner. According to mimamsa scriptures are the only source to determine dharma that prescribes sacred and moral duties. This school of worship through work is due to rishi Jaimini who considered the world as eternally dynamic. Rishi Jaimini is believed to have lived between 3rd and 1st century B.C. He is said to have summed up the general rules of Nyaya doctrine following the tenets of Vedas. The Mimamsa doctrine of Jaimini was composed in 12 chapters. The main purpose of the scripture was to reestablish the authority of Vedas which was questioned by Buddhism. It recommends unshakeable faith in Vedas. One has to perform yajnas or the fire sacrifices regularly as prescribed in Vedas. Belief in the power of the mantras and yajnas is essential. Performing vedic rituals is considered as Dharma, the duty of the house holder. While accepting all other schools of vedic thought, it was felt that sufficient emphasis was not laid on right action. There is no liberation unless freedom is achieved from desire and selfishness. It was argued that to work for liberation or moksha is also a desire. Even that desire has to be renounced. It is by following injunctions of Vedas only then one may attain liberation. Mimamsa deals with the ritualistic commands in Vedas.

Mimamsa sutras or aphorisms describe the different sacrifices and their significance. It explains about the mysterious transcendental power that is produced by an appropriately performed sacrificial rtiual called 'apurva'. The power is experienced mostly after death only, by the performer of the sacrifice.

The Vedas are eternal and are not created even by the Divine. Vedas exist as the sacred communication to the world for moral and spiritual order. Since the world is eternal the idea of God appears as superfluous. Jaimini rejected the idea of treating a deity as the creator in both word and meaning. He considered the relationship between word, its meaning and the relationship between the two as eternal. This leads one to treat mimamsa as theory of speech. The sacred word uttered as 'sabda' (sound) has three cannotations when a sacrifice is performed; 'mantra' the sacred utterance of the ritual, 'vidhi' directives for action and 'ardhvada' the hidden reality underlying it. Mimamsa remained as a guide for the performance of rituals to the twice born till todate. Poorva mimamsa tried to explain the mystical meaning of the various ritual acts and the implements used in them. There are two schools of poorva mimamsa. They are the Bhatta's (Kumarila Bhatta) and Prabhakara's schools which have only minor differences.

(vi) Uttara Mimamsa or Brahmasutras

Sutras, also called aphorisms are very brief statements with least possible number of letters containing complete meaning without any ambiguity. Uttara Mimamsa, a darsana or a pathway to understand the absolute Truth, 'Brahmasutras', consists of 555 aphorisms. They are divided into four parts namely:

Samanvaya Adhyaya,
Avirodha Adhyaya,
Sadhana Adhyaya and
Phala Adhyaya.

In all, there are 192 sections that contain these 555 aphorisms. To understand the contents in Vedas clearly one must acquire proficiency in the six sciences considered briefly earlier namely: Sikha, Vyakaran, Chandas, Nirukta, Kalpa and Jyotish. To properly comprehend and correlate the apparently contradicting ideas presented in Vedas, study of mimamsa is essential. Poorva Mimamsa stresses the need to perform rituals and sacrifices as ordained in Vedas (Samhitas and Brahmanas). But, they result in temporary benefits only and do not lead to liberation of the soul. The first few sutras from Samanvaya explain as follows:

- An enquiry into Brahma is made.
- Brahma is the source of the Universe.
- Scripture is the only source to understand Brahma.
- The purpose of scripture is to reveal Brahma.
- Pradhana (of Sankhya) is not Brahma.
- Ananda (bliss Supreme) is Brahma
- The attributes of Brahma can be seen in the sun and in the eye.
- Akasha (space) is Brahma.
- Breath is also Brahma.
- Light is Brahma.
- Prana is Brahma.
- Mental sheath is Brahma.
- The eater is Brahma.
- The individual and the Supreme Self that entered into the cave of the heart too is Brahma.
- The person seen in the eye is Brahma.

- The internal ruler of the body who controls all other gods in the body is Brahma.
- The one who possesses the qualities such as invisibility, indivisibility, etc., is Brahma.
- Vaisvanara is Brahma.
- Brahma is the resting place for everything. Bhuma, the state beyond deep sleep is Brahma. The imperishable is Brahma.
- The one to be realized is Brahma.
- The smallest space is Brahma.
- Sun, moon and stars are illuminated by Brahma. Light by virtue of illumination is Brahma.
- The Self consisting of knowledge is Brahma.

Nature is not the cause for the world. The whole universe is Brahma only. Brahma is unchahgeable. The Innerself in all is Brahma. Jeeva, the individual soul is not the innerself. Deverse or apparently conflicting aspects are correlated and misinterpretations are removed in this first part of the book called Samanvaya.

In the second part of the book called Avirodha or non conflicting nature, the vedantic tenets stand unrefuted.

In the third part Sadhna means are revealed. Upasana (worship), Jnana (knowledge of the spirit), and karma (rituals), and upanishads are the various means. For both meditation and worship Brahma with attributes becomes necessary. For the renounced rituals are not needed.

In Phala Adhyaya the fruits of Sadhana are discussed. With right knowledge liberation is here and now only. Moksha or salvation is not a thing to be acquired. It is ever present.

There is considerable debate on the prerequisites of acquiring knowledge of Brahma. According to Sri Adi Sankaracharya, it is necessary that one must achieve the following four requisites. They are:

- Discrimination between the real and the unreal,
- Detachment from pleasures, here and hereafter,
- Acquisition of six types of disciplining qualities – internal control, external control, forbearance, equanimity of mind, mendicancy and faith
- And an intense desire to achieve liberation.

CHAPTER 12

The Smritis

Smriti actually means recollection or remembering. This means that we follow in our daily life a code of conduct that is according to the spirit of Vedas. There are 18 smritis or Dharamasastras (laws for right conduct) that are mentioned in this context. They are:

- Manu smriti
- Yajnavalkya smriti
- Sankha smriti
- Likhita smriti
- Parasara smriti
- Angirasa smriti
- Apasthambha smriti
- Vyasa smriti
- Daksha smriti
- Vishnu smriti
- Samvarta smriti
- Brihaspati smriti
- Atri smriti
- Katyayana smriti
- Aushanasa smriti
- Harita smriti.
- Gautama smriti
- Yama smriti

These are the age old law codes or tenets that defined Sanathana Dharma. Smritis are based on Srutis or Vedas. The laws that regulate the Hindu society are codified into smrits. As Hindu society changed from time to time new smritis have emerged from time to time. These smritis were handed over to the people by the highly learned and wise sages of the past to protect dharma and preserve mankind. The important smritis are due to

Manu, Yagnyavalkya, Sankha-Likhita and Parasara. However, Parasara, father of Veda Vyasa said

> " *Krite tu Dharmastretayaam Gautamo Smritah*
>
> *Dwapare Sankha Likhita Kalau Parasarah Smritah* "
>
> Which means that -
>
> Manu smriti was for Satya yuga,
>
> Gautama smriti was for Treta yuga,
>
> Sankha-Likhita smriti was for Dwapara yuga and
>
> Parasara smriti is for the present Kaliyuga.

It is noteworthy that the highly resilient Hindu society has been changing its codes of conduct along with social changes occurring over yugas. This flexibility is the greatest asset of the Hindu religion. Most of Hindu laws were replaced by Parliamentary Statutes, such as 'The Hindu Marriage Act' (1955), 'The Hindu Succession Act' (1956) , 'The Hindu Adoption and Maintenance Act' (1956) etc. But the Indian legal experts consulted several of these smritis such as Yajnavalkya smriti before finalizing the bills and obtained the sanction of the Parliament. Mitaksara a commentary on Yajnavalkya smriti by Vijneswara and Dayabhaga a digest of all smritis played an important role in finalizing these legal matters.

Manu Smriti

Manu smriti contains 2605 codes of which only 1214 are supposed to be authentic and the rest of 1471 are the interpolation of the text. It is the considered opinion of Dr. Ambedkar that one Brigu wrote it at the time of Sunga king Pushyamitra to curb Buddhism. Noted historian Romila Thaper, however contradicts this. According to Chanakya of Artha Satra there were no social laws made binding on people at that time (300 B.C). All these smritis might have come between 200 B.C. and 200 C.E. Megasthanese, the Greek historian and traveler mentioned that people around Mathura follwed Bhgavad Gita as rule book. Manusmriti has been highlighted by William Jones who translated it from Sanskrit into English in the year 1794 C.E. Dharma sastras were only norms and social obligations and requirements for rituals. As Manusmriti is extensive and exhaustive and widely known some of the salient features will be presented here.

The universe existed in the shape of darkness, unknowable in deep sleep. The Indiscernible and the Eternal created first waters and in it Hiranyagarbha, the Golden egg. From that He Himself was born as Brahma, the progenitor of the world. Purusha, was then the first born who came out. Later, mind and egoism the self consciousness were born. Living creatures came into existence. Fire, wind and sun as well as the Vedas were given. To begin creation, action pairs of opposites were formed. He Himself split into male and female. Ten great sages - Marichi, Atri, Angirasa, Pulastya, Pulaha, Kratu, Praketas, Vasishta, Bhrigu, and Narada, were created through meditation. They created seven Manus and many other sages. Cycles of action and inactivity were created. The Absolute Reality, the Imperishable one then taught sacred laws to Brahma who in turn taught to Marichi and others. Bhrigu taught to all other sages these sacred laws and that information is Manusmriti.

To act solely from the desire to obtain rewards is not noble.

Sacrifices mentioned in Vedas can be performed in countries where there is prosperity. Excessive eating is considered prejudicial to health, to fame and to bliss in heaven. It prevents spiritual upliftment.

The essence of Vedas is condensed into the three primal sounds A –U – M. and the three Vyahrutis Bhuh, Bhuvah, and Svah.

There are no forbidden days for reciting vedic hymns, since it is an everlasting sacrifice offered to Brahma.

Unless one is asked one must not explain anything.

One must not answer a question put improperly.

Even in dire distress a teacher should not give his knowledge to an undeserving disciple. It is recommended that his knowledge may die along with him rather than being given to unworthy disciples.

Women are considered as a source of seduction. Hence, wise men are required to be always on guard in the company of females.

Obedience to teacher, father and mother is ordained.

Possessing several wives is not decried.

He who possesses faith may receive pure learning even from a man of lower caste.

Highest law can be learned from the lowest caste person.

Excellent wife can be taken even from a base family.

One should serve the teacher as long as the instruction lasts.

Where women are honored there the Gods are pleased.

Happiness prevails in a house where the wife and husband live harmoniously.

Humans commit sins everyday using the hearth, the grinding stone, the broom, the mortar and the water vessel. That is to say that several seen and unseen life forms perish while these items are used in daily life. To expiate these sins five daily sacrifices were prescribed. They are spiritual studies and teaching, offering food and water as 'Tarpana' to manes or Pitris, burning oblations to Gods as sacrifice , giving food to birds, insects, worms and others, and giving hospitality to guests. (Brahma, Pitru, Deva Bhuta, Atithi Yajnas)

Perfectly contended disposition is necessary for happiness. The root of happiness is contentment.

Prosperity through unrighteousness is only temporary. The unrighteous will perish ultimately.

One should not quarrel with members of the family, relatives and even with the servants (slaves). Rules governing bringing up of children, in tne performance of routine duties, in behavior, with respect to elders are all well laid out.

For entering into the highest state of existence one must possess contentment, forgiveness, self control, abstention from unrighteous acts, purification, wisdom, knowledge of soul, truthfulness, control of anger and control of organs.

Administrative rules, dispensation of justice, and settlement of disputes were all considered. For some offences harsh punishments were prescribed.

Mutual fidelity until death was ordained for couples.

For surviving at any cost in dire circumstances, even eating forbidden food from unclean sources is not considered a sin.

Protecting the cow is considered a great act.

Action springs from mind. Mind is instigates for all actions.

He who recognizes Self, and the same Self in all created beings, becomes equal minded to all and enters the highest state.

Yajnavalkya smriti: There are 1010 slokas in this smriti. This smriti is systematically classified into three major parts. They are Achara kanda or religious rights section, Vyavaharika kanda or judicial procedure section, and Prayaschitta kanda or penance section. Thus in this smriti religion and law are separated, which is a considerable advancement towards secularism. This smriti is shorter and liberal towards women than Manusmriti. This smriti is hailed and followed by judiciary in several cases.

Sankha smriti: This smriti consists of 18 Adhyaayas or sections. The first two sections explain the obligatory duties of a Brahmin boy in 20 slokas. Third section deals with the mode of observance of celibacy in 12 slokas. The fourth and fifth sections deal with the marriage process and the duties of householder in 33 slokas. The sixth pertains to withdrawal from worldly life, that is sanyasa dharma in 7 slokas, while the seventh one explains in 34 slokas the mode of pranayama, dharana and dhyana aspects of yoga or control of mind and body. Sections 8, 9 and 10 contain details about cleansing of body by bathing and initiation into worship in 57 slokas. The performance of Gayatri worship was considered in 31 slokas in 12th section. Sections 13, 14, 15. 16 and 17 deal with several penances in 165 slokas. Finally the last section explains the method to be followed for fasting in 16 slokas.

Likhita smriti: This smriti explains the rules governing certain sacrifices known as "Ishta poorthi", and the sixteen penances to be performed by Hindus at Gaya for pitris in 96 slokas.

Parasara smriti: The first chapter deals with the duties assigned to Brahmins, Ksatriyas, Vaisyas and Sudras. The second one explains the conduct of married life. Methods of purification from birth and death is the content for the third. Chapters 4, 5, 6, 8, 9 and 10 suggest various penances for evil deeds and sins committed including killing of cow and for those committed inadvertently. Cleaning processes are discussed in chapter 7. How to avoid nightmares is the topic of 11th chapter. Finally the last part proposes norms for eating and for earning money. In fact, religion is highlighted as earning money by just means. In all there are 583 slokas in this smriti.

Angirasa smriti: In 72 slokas this smriti explains penances for various sins committed.

Apasthambha smriti: There are ten chapters in this smriti consisting of 198 slokas They generally explain the procedures for enforcing right conduct and penances for various types of sins and offences.

Vyasa smriti: In this smriti the procedures for all the four castes of people to observe right conduct are enunciated. In all 16 different samskaras or religious ceremonies are detailed. The process of conduct of marriage is described. Cleansing processes and householder's duties are also explained.

Daksha smriti: In seven Adhyayas or chapters comprising 208 slokas Dakhsa smriti presents the stipulations for people of all castes for right conduct and householders' duties.

Vishnu smriti: This smriti is an exhortation of Maharshi Saunaka to Yudhishtira and is more devotional and philosophical when compared to other smritis which are more about sins and penances. Lord Vishnu is of course, the deity to whom the devotion is directed. In all there are 113 slokas in this smriti.

Samvarta smriti: In 227 slokas this smriti explains the importance and mode of observing celibacy for those pursuing vedic studies. It discusses further the right and the wrong conduct in daily life and the procedures of compensation for any offences or violations committed. The various penances for the acts of breaking the moral and ethical codes are also contained in this smriti.

Harita smriti: There are 8 parts or adhyayas in this smriti with 2530 slokas. A king who was a great devotee of Lord Vishnu received this smriti. The intial chapters deal with the procedures related to 'panchasamskaras' or five ritualistic ceremonies for vedic disciples. Later the procedures connected with worshipping the Lord are detailed. The various modes of conducting ceremonies for Lord Vishnu are instructed. Also ordained are the several penances for committed unforgivable sins.

Aushanasa smriti: This is also called 'Sukrasamhita' and contains 51 slokas. It explains the duties identified for all the four classes of citizens.

Katyayana smriti: This smriti is in 29 parts and has 480 slokas. It explains the procedures involved in wearing the 'sacred thread' called 'yajnopaveeta' and details about the various rites and purification procedures. It contains also mantras for worship at sun rise and sun set times and for midday worship, marriage procedures, duties for women, several rites to be performed at the time of birth and death. Rites for the ancestors and penances are also specified.

Atri smriti: This smriti with five chapters is short with 140 slokas and different from other smritis in the sense that it explains 'yoga' for acquisition of knowledge. Meditation on 'Gayatri' mantra or hymn is recommended for enlightenment. The importance of 'Pranayama' or breath control and 'tapas' or deep meditation are highlighted. Some penances too are presented.

Brihaspati smriti: Through 81 slokas this smriti brings out the beneficial facts concerning land donation to the poor and the deserving.

Gautama smriti: There are 29 'prakaranas' or chapters in this smriti. Some chapters are in prose while others are in poetic or sloka form This smriti deals with a variety of issues concerning daily life of individuals and society. Duties prescribed and proscribed for citizens of all castes, norms concerning family life, householders' duties, observance of celibacy, performance of actions according to Vedas are discussed. Paying attention to proper duties, several methods of worship, are detailed. Women's obligations at specific periods are mentioned. All sorts of penances for various kinds of sins committed are clearly laid down. This is an important smriti that defines right conduct.

Yama smriti: This smriti consists of 78 slokas and ordains penances for several types of sins.

The smritis came into existence at different points of time and are by several sages and they reflect to some extent the social conditions that existed then. Many of them may not be either applicable now or may be even irrelevant under the present conditions. But the core of the Vedic spirit, Sanathana Dharma as enshrined in these smritis remain forever the doctrines for humankind. Truthfulness, nonviolence and righteousness will remain the edifice on which civilizations have to rest.

CHAPTER 13
Itihasas

These contain history of the past that incorporate practice of dharma in daily life. The heros in ithihasas are supposed to be role models for emulation. Dharma or righteousness is the main theme of these scriptures and are meant for the masses. They are briefly explained.

Ramayana

It contains 24,000 verses divided into 7 kandas. Literally Ramayana means the journey of Rama. He is the role model for Indians. Historians dated Ramayana to have been written some time between 500 B.C to 100 B.C by maharshi Valmiki. But, tradition dates it to much earlier time. The epic is written in 32 syllable Anushtubh chandas or meter. The seven kandas – Bala, Ayodhya, Aranya, Kishkindha, Sundara, Lanka, and Uttara kandas describe the life journey of Rama believed to be the incarnation of Lord Vishnu. It is said that Rama is Dharma incarnate.

"Ramo Vigrahavan Dharma" is the saying. Rama is personification of righteousness. Rama is said to possess 16 qualities that made Him and Ramayana unique. Ramayana is the first literary work in the world and is called 'Adikavya'. The gunas or characterizing features of Rama are - valour, righteousness, truthfulness, self confidence, good conduct, compassion, scholarship, ability, pleasant countenance, courage, ability to control anger, brilliance, nonexistence of jealousy, gratitude etc. There is no Indian who is not aware of the story of Rama.

Yogavasishta

Yogavasisshta contains 32,000 verses or słokas and is a part of Brahmandapurana. Authored by Veda Vyasa, it is a voluminous epic presenting stories within stories. While Bhagavadgita is meant for a student like Arjuna who was caught up in delusion and "moha", or attachment to his relations and teachers against whom he had to fight, Yogavasishta is for a student like Rama who developed dispassion after completing his education and after observing the world outside in a critical manner. Thus it is for a serious student seeking the true meaning of this world and life. Valmiki narrates the story of Ramayana to sage Bharadwaja which is contained in 24,000 slokas. When Bharadwaja requests Brahma to explain about liberation, Brahma prompts him to go back to Valmiki for the same and seek the path to liberation from him. When approached, Valmiki describes the path to liberation which is the subject matter of Yogavasishta. Originally this was revealed to Rama by sage Vasishta. Rama developed a strong dispassion at the end of his education and after a pilgrimage that he undertook along with his brothers and ministers. Then, sage Vasishta explains Rama the essence of philosophy. Rama understands that in real life men were trying to grab things which are only images in mirror and in truth had no existence. The teachings of Vasishta form six chapters of Yogavasishta. They are:

1. Vairagya prakarana (chapter of dispassion),
2. Mumukshu prakarana (desire for liberation),
3. Utpatti prakarana (chapter of creation),
4. Sthiti prakarana (chapter of sustenance),
5. Upasamharana prakarana (chapter of dissolution) and
6. Nirvana or Jivanmukti prakarana (liberation while living).

It is after this that the enlightened Rama along with his brother Lakshmana accompanied sage Viswamitra to protect his sacrifice that ultimately resulted in his marriage with Sita.

Mahabharata

The epic Mahabharata, in fact, was originally called 'Jaya' meaning victory and was written by Veda Vyasa. It explains human values and goals such as dharma (duties), artha (purposes), kama (desires and pleasures) and moksha (liberation). Further, the interrelationship between individual, society and the world, working of karma (the results and consequences of past works) were discussed. In course of time it was expanded into 24,000 verses and formed the core of Mahabharata. At this stage it was recited by sage Vaisampayana and was called 'Bharata'. Experts feel that further expansion of the epic poem took place between fifth century B.C. and fourth century A.D. It contained more than 74,000 verses with more than 1.8 million words. The story in this epic poem concerns Kuru dynasty that was very influential during second and first millennium B.C.E. The period of Mahabharata war is differently speculated. Mahapadmananda of Nanda dynasty is said to have acceeded to his throne in 382 B.C. The time between Parikshit the grandson of Arjuna, the hero of the war and Mahapadmananda is calculated as 1050 years. This puts the occurrence of the war to about 1400 B.C. Famed astronomer Arybhatta of 6th century suggested from his calculations based on astronomical references as 18

February 3102 B.C. Kalhana and others opined that the war took place around 2449 B.C. Archeological finds attributed to that period suggests a much recent date for the war.

Harivamsa

Harivamsa is supposed to have been composed around first or second century A.D. It consists of 16,375 verses. This great classic describes the early life story of Lord Krishna and his various activities involving the people of Brindavan. Some people consider it as an extension of Mahabharata.

The principles of dharma as derived from vedic culture are explained for the benefit of the common man in an elegant and simple way in itihasas.

CHAPTER 14

The Puranas

The Puranas are similar to itihasas. But all the 18 puranas possess a common feature in the sense that they deal with cosmology, secondary creation, manvantaras, history and geneology of kings . The purpose of puranas is to promote vedic knowledge among masses. These eighteen puranas are:

Agni purana, Bhagavatha purana, Bhavishya purana, Brahma purana, Brahmanda purana, Brahmavaivarth purana, Garuda purana, Kurma purana, Linga purana, Markandeya purana, Matsya purana, Naradeeya purana, Padma purana , Shiva purana, Skanda purana, Vamana purana, Varaha purana, and Vishnu purana.

Of these Bhagavatha purana is the most popular purana. Puranas are said to belong to 3rd to 12th centuries of Christian era. Most of the puranas were supposed to have been compiled during the Gupta period (320 -500 C.E.). In the following another important purana Vayu purana is also included in addition to the 18 major puranas.

Agni Purana: This purana contains 15,400 verses. Various avataras or incarnations of Lord Vishnu are described in ths scripture. The stories of Rama and Krishna are elaborately retold. This purana is a narration of Fire god Agni to sage Vasishta. This 383 chapter book includes diverse topics such as cosmology, earth and stars, history, warfare, law, medicine, martial arts, ritual bathing, temple repair, idols and their installation, astrology, astronomy, sacred water spots for bathing, fire place and mudras. All the 10 avatars of Vishnu are detailed and the summary of Ramayana and the complete story of Mahabharata are narrated once again. In this purana the abstract of Harivamsa is found in the 12th chapter. In the 16th chapter Buddha and Kalki avataras are included. The gist of Bhagavadgita is also present in this purana. The consecration of a temple also featured in this purana. The description of the universe 'Bhuvanakosha' and the geography of India and the world are explained. Worship of Surya, Ganesh, Skanda, Linga, Devi and Ganas of Lord Shiva are to be found in this purana. Matters pertaining to Vedas including phonetics, grammar, figures of speech, and Sanskrit dramas are another set of topics to be found here. Raja yoga, hatha yoga and human anatomy are also discussed. Reference to Self realization is also made.

Bhagavatha purana: This most important purana contains 15000 verses. It is considered to be the essence of all vedic literature and Vedanta. It forms the basis for Vaishnava theology. It talks about creation, cosmology and the lineage of great rishis. In this narration by sage Suta to other sages the avataras of Lord Vishnu are elegantly explained. The life history of Krishna is told in a vivid manner. The end of Kaliyuga and the destruction that was about to occur has been mentioned. Time and interplanetary travel are explained indicating their effect on aging. The development of embryo in the womb is also discussed. The Divine Source, the withdrawal of cosmic creation and liberation are also narrated.

Bhavishya purana: In this 14,500 verse purana there are four parts – Brahma parva, Madhyama parva, Pratisarga parva, and Uttara parva.

Brahma parva contains brahminical ceremonies, feasts, duties of castes. The duties of women are also described. Worshipping of Brahma, Ganesha, Skanda, and Sun in Saka Dvipa are included.

Madhyama Parva contains tantric elements.

Pratisarga Parva contains the names of Adam, Noah, Yakuta, Taimurlong, Nadirshah, Akbar, Jayachandra and even Calcutta and Parliament. Mention is also made of prophets Christ, Moses and Mohammed.

Uttara Parva consists of few legends, myths in addition to certain religious rites.

Brahma Purana: This purana consists of 24,000 verses in two parts. Initially Lord Brahma narrated this purana to sage Marichi. At the time of the purana it was a narration by Lomaharshana to rishis at Nimesaranya.

The first part or 'purvaa bhag' deals with the story of the creation of the cosmos as well as the life and deeds of Rama and Krishna.

The second part or 'Uttara bhag' describes a sacred place called Purusshottam Tirtha.

A number of chapters are devoted to temples dedicated to Sun, Shiva and Jagannath in the Indian state of Orissa. This indicates that this purana was composd during the 13th century of Christian era. Towards the end yoga, a contemplative devotion to Lord Vishnu has been explained. It also contains an account of the river Balaja, (probably Banas river in Marwar) and its sanctity.

Brahmanda purana: This purana has only 12,000 verses. The famous Adhyatma Ramayana is a part of this purana. It also contains 'Lalitha Sahasranama' a powerful prayer to the Goddess Sakti, the creative, sustaining and destrying force in 1000 words. There are in all seven parts in this purana. An account of creation, time and Kalpa are given. A description of the geography of Jambu dvipa, Bharat varsha and other land masses like Anu dvipa and Ketumala varsha are included in this purana. Dynasties of Bharata, Deva, Prithu, Rishi and Agni are detailed. The formation of this world or 'Prapanch' from the Golden egg or 'Hiranyagarbha' forms part of it. The story of Radha and Krishna is also given in this purana. The avatar or incarnation of the Lord as Parasurama and description of Vedangas are the other important topics in this purana.

Brahmavaivarta Purana: This 18,000 verse purana contains the story of the creation of universe and all beings as in other puranas. The history of the different goddesses, life and deeds of Ganesha and Krishna are the other contents. Goddesses are the manifestation of nature or 'prakriti'. Lord Krishna living in Goloka with Raseswari Radha created the universe. He created Brahma, Vishnu and Shiva for creation, preservation and dissoulution of the universes. The legend of Radha-Krishna is vividly presented in this purana.

Garuda Purana: This purana consists of 19,000 verses. The purva kanda or the first part consists of 234 chapters and describes the various incarnations of the Supreme lord. They are Kumara, Varaha, Devarshi, Nara-Narayan, Kapila, Dattatreya, Vishnu as son of Akuti and Ruchi, Urukrama (also Vishnu) as son of Nabhi and Meru, Prithu, Matsya (as saviour of Vaivasvat manu), Kurma, Dhanvantari, Mohini, Narasimha, Vamana, Parasurama, Vedavyasa (as son of Parasara and Satyavati), Narada, Rama, Krishna, Buddha, Kalki and many more.

The later part of this purana in 45 chapters describes life after death.

Kurma Purana: In this purana of 17,000 verses Lord Vishnu Himself explains Kurma avatar or incarnation. There are four parts of this purana called – Brahmi samhita 6000 verses each of four padas, Sauri samhita of 4000 verses each of five padas, Vaishnavi samhita with 2000 verses but each of six padas and Bhagavati samhita containing 5000 verses of four padas each. It is again divided into two parts called purvabhag and uttarbhag or the first and the later parts.

Linga Purana: There are two parts in this 17,000 verse purana. The origin of linga and its worship are clarified. Creation, cosmos, 'Kamadhenu', the divine cow that fulfills all the desires and Lord Shiva's marriage are other subjects narrated. The avataras or incarnations of Varaha and Narasimha are discussed. Reference is made to Surya and Soma. It explains the prominence of Vishnu, creative activity of Brahma and the features of Shiva. It describes the seven islands in the world. Mount Meru and other mountains are described. The assignment of divine powers to several deities by Brahma is given. Dynasties of Yadu, Andhak are detailed. The story of Jalandhar and Upamanyu are narrated. The significance of Guru and the importance of mantras (metered verses) are explained. The types of yoga are introduced. The installation of Linga is detailed. The undivided causal principle Shiva is worshipped as Linga. Linga is sexless, shapeless, colourless, odourless, changeless and imperceptible.

Markandeya Purana: This purana of 9,000 verses is the answer to the four questions put to sage Markandeya by sage Jaimini. This purana narrates the genealogies of puranic dynasties. It gives a detailed account of the 14 manvantaras. In this purana Devimahatmyam, the glory of the Goddess Durga is highlighted in chapter 34. This purana is neutral to both Vishnu and Shiva.

Matsya Purana: This purana of 14000 verses is considered to be the oldest purana. The avatar of Vishnu as fish is explained. According to this purana emperor Satyavrata became a manu and progenitor of Aryans. A great deluge was said to have occurred two billion years ago and Lord Vishnu as a fish or Matsya guided and rescued Manu, his family and others. Vedas and vedic way of life were revealed. The kingdom Dravida mentioned in this purana probably consisted of East Africa, Madagaskar, Southern India, Southeast Asia and Australia as per the opinion of some experts. Manu was the son of Sun god.

Naradeeya purana: This purana of 25,000 verses is in the form of a dialogue between sage Narada and Sanatkumara. Various places of pilgrimage, their locations and significance are explained. It contains the story of Markandeya, the son of Mrikandu. In this story Lord Vishnu grants Markandeya life till the end of the present cosmic cycle. Saunaka along with 26,000 sages and their disciples reach the hermitage of sage Suta at Siddhasramaa in Nimesaranya to hear this purana from Suta. Some of the important stories narrated were about Sondasa, Bali, Vamana, Bhagirath, Sumati and Ganga. The importance of several deity oriented worship and rituals (or 'Vratas') were also explained. This purana details time and its units. The smallest unit is 'nimesha'.

It is given that the following relations exist :

15 nimeshas form one 'Kashtha'.

30 kashthas form one 'kala'.

30 kalas form one 'kshana'

6 kshanas form one 'danda'

2 dandas form one 'muhurta'

30 muhurtas form one day.

30 days form one month or' masa'

15 days form one 'paksha'

2 pakshas form one month

2 months form one 'ritu'

3 ritus form one 'ayana'.

2 ayanas form one year or 6 ritus.

1 human year is one divine day.

12,000 divine years form one 'mahayuga'.

2000 mahayugas form one day for Brahma.

100 years of Brahma form one day for Vishnu.

Markandeya floated in dissolution one complete night of Brahma which is called 'Kalpa'. This purana lists out the 14 regions of the universe, the seven great islands or dvipas and the sacred rivers on earth.

Padma purana: This is another great purana of 55,000 verses. It is also in the form of a dialogue between sage Pulastya and Bhishma, the famous Kuru prince of Mahabharata. In the first part the importance of religion is explained. In the second part earth and its geography, and in the third part cosmos, creation and India are interpreted. In part four the life and deeds of Rama is highlighted. The last and fifth part is in the form of a dialogue between Shiva and Parvati about universe, cosmos and religion.

At the time of narration the world was in the form of a Padma or lotus and all the occurrences of that time are described. Some recensions contain a sixth part describing 'kriya yoga sara' a treatise on the practice of devotion.

Srishti kanda contains the importance of Pushkar lake (near Ajmer). Ugrasrava, the son of Lomaharshana was the narrator. Brahma appeared in a lotus at the time of creation. The earlier part of the chapter gives an account of cosmogony, genealogy of the patriarchal families as well as manvantaras and royal dynasties.

Bhumikanda describes earth, geography and history of that time. It also narrates the stories of Prithu, Yayati and others. It contains the mixed description of several legends which are common to some other puranas as well. Some holy places for taking sin absolving bath (tirthas) are also mentioned

Swargakanda contains creation and cosmos. It explains Jambudvipa and India. It also gives the relative position of the several worlds (lokas) Vaikuntha. It is placed above all of them. Patriarch Daksha and his famous sacrifice was also included.

Patalakanda explains the metaphysics of religion. Vishnusahasranama and Rama sahasranama are also found in this part. Ugrasrava Sauti (sage Suta) narrates the story of Rama to an assembly of rishis in this part. He also details the avatar of Lord Krishna. Patala is the region of snake gods. The merits of Vishnu worship are highlighted. Shiva explains to Parvati in this part the mode of Tantrik worship of Narayana.

It also describes the yugas. Each manvantara is explained to about 71 chaturyugas. Chaturyuga is a set of Satya, Treta, Dwapara and Kali yugas. One manvantara is about 30,67,20,000 years. One day of Brahma is equal to 14 x 30,67,20,000 = 4,29,40,80,000 years. Brahma's life span is 100 years. He created rishis, Bhrigu, Pulah, Kratu, Angira, Marichi, Daksha, Atri and Vasishta and wanted them to create people but they refused. Then at Brahma's request Rudra created Manu and Satarupa for the same purpose. They had four sons Priyavrata, Uttanapada, Prasuti and Aakuti. The story of the churning of ocean and the birth of Lakshmi as well as the story of Sati are to be found in this purana. Eleven Rudras, Ajaikpad, Ahirbudhnya, Virupaksh, Raivat, Har, Bahuroop, Tryambak, Savitra, Jayant, Pinaki and Aparajit lead 84 crore Rudra ganas, the followers of Rudra. This purana also includes the stories of Ganesha, Kartikeya, Bhaskali (Bali), Yayati, and Pridhu of Sun dynasty. The significance of Gayatri mantra, Rudraksha, Tulasi and Amalaka are explained. The stories of Rama, Krishna, Jarasandh, Rukmini, Anirudh, Parasuram will be found in this purana. Further, the avatars of Matsya, Kurma, Nrisimha, Vamana are narrated. The exit of the avatar of Krishna is described.

Shivapurana: This purana of 24,000 verses is dedicated to Lord Shiva. It was said that originally Shiva purana contained 12 samhitas and 1,00,000 verses. Vedavyasa reorganized the material into 24,000 verses and told to Romaharshana his disciple. There are several recensions in existence. The popular samhitas are Jnanasamhita (78 ch.), Vidyesvarasamhita (12 ch.), Kailasasamhita (12 ch.) Sanatkumarasamhita (59 ch), Vayaveeyasamhita (30 ch. in two parts) and Dharmasamhita(65 ch.). Some other recensions contain Vainayaka, Matr, Uma Rudra, Satarudra, Kotirudra and other smritis dedicated to Lord Shiva, Goddess Parvati, Skanda and Ganesha.

Skandapurana: This is really a major purana containing 81,100 verses in seven parts or Khandas. They are Mahesvarakhanda, Vishnukhanda, Brahmakhanda, Kasikhanda Avantyakhanda, Nagarakhanda, and Prabhasakhanda.

Mahesvarakhanda contains exposition of the glory of various places, persons and months, namely, Kedarakanda, Kaumarikakanda, Arunachalamahatmyam. Vishnukhanda consists of Venkatachalamahatmya, Purushothamakshetramahatmya, Badarikasramamahatmya, Kartikamasamahatmya, Margasiramasamahatmya, Bhagavathamahatmya, Vaisakhamasamahatmya, Ayodhyamahatmya, and Vasudevamahatmya.

Brahmakhanda similarly describes the greatness of Setu, Dharmaranya, and Brahmottarakanda.

Kasikhanda includes description of the importance of Avanti and the greatness of Chaturasitilinga. It also contains Revakhanda. Nagarakhanda describes the holiness of several places. Prabhasakhanda explains the sanctity of the places called Prabhasa, Vastrapathaka and Dwaraka.

The story of Daksha, Churning of the ocean, Parvati and Shiva, and the birth of Kartikeya, the killing of Tarakasura, Pralambasura, Sumbha, Nisumbha and Mahishasura are included in this purana. Trisanku and Visvamitra story also exist in this purana. Many untraced stories are attributed to this purana.

Vamanapurana: This purana is dedicated to Vamana Avatar of Lord Vishnu. But, it praises both Vishnu and Shiva. Sage Narada asks Pulastya to explain about Vamana incarnation of Vishnu. It contains the stories of Daksha' sacrifice, Demon king Andhak, Sukesi son of Vidyutkesi, Nar-Narayan, Prahlad, Mahishasura, Chand and Munda demons, Durga, Kuru and Kurukshetra, Bali, Vamanas' avatar, marriage of Shiva and Uma, Kartikeya, Taraka, Ritudhwaj, Killing of Mura by Vishnu, Andhaka's death, Shukracharya, Sanjeevani, Marutganas, Upamanyu, Sreedama, Gajendra and the crocodile and other stories. Saraswti river and Goddess Saraswati stotras are also the other highlights in this purana . Bali's dispatch to the nether world Patala concludes the purana.

Vayupurana: It is basically not among the main 18 puranas. However, it is an important upapurana and hence it is included here. It is consists of two parts. This purana was recited during the reign of Adhisima Krishna. Janamejaya was the son of Parikshit and Shatanika was the son of Janamejaya. Shatanika's son was Ashwamedhadatta whose son was Adhisima Krishna. He ruled the country very well. Sacrifices and rituals were performed regularly. Narmada river was described in detail indicating that the region of Malva was ruled over by Adhisima Krishna. In all, this purana contains 112 chapters. According to this purana Nimesharanya was located on the banks of Gomati river (present Sitapur district of Uttar Pradesh). The first part consists of both pratisirga and upodghata , while the second part covers anusarga and upasamhara. The general characteristics of puranas – legends, stories, mahatmyas or divine characteristics of places, waters, mountains and others as well as stotras or prayer songs and rituals are all present in this purana. The geographic description of India or Bharatvarsha with its rivers, mountains and regions is given. The story of churning of the ocean for Ambrosia is detailed. The killing of the demon Dhundhu by Kuvalasva is described. The story of Trishanku (Satyavrata), Sagara, Pururava and Urvasi, Yayati, Kartavirya Arjuna form part of this purana. Sutas are according to this purana descendents of couples where father was Kshatriya and mother was Brahmana.

The seven rishis, and Indra change every manvantara. The origin of mankind was attributed to Brahma creating Swayambhu Manu who, along with Satarupa had Priyavrata, and Uttanapada as sons and Prasuti and Aakuti as daughters. Prasuti married Daksha and gave birth to 24 daughters who were married to Shiva and other great rishis, Bhrigu, Marichi, Angira, Pulastya, Pulaha, Kratu, Atri and Vasishta. All the other 13 were married to Dharma, the son of Brahma. As per this purana Yoga was taught by Shiva and consists of pranayama, dhyana, pratyahara, dharana, and smarana.

One kalpa is explained as 4320,000,000 years for this period is a day for Brahma. One thousand kalpas form a year to Brahma. 8000 such years form a yuga for Brahma. Such 1000 yugas are called a saravanna. 2000 saravannas, called a trivrita constitutes the life period of Brahma.

The measurement of distances starts with anguli (finger) and the largest unit was given as yojana. 10 angulis form one pradesha, which is the distance between thumb and extended index finger. Distance between thumb extended to middle finger is called one tata. Distance between thumb and extended ring finger is called gokarna. Likewise, the distance between thumb and extended little finger is called vitasti. 12 angulus form one vitasti. 21 angulis form one ratni. 24 angulis form one hasta. Four hastas are one dhanu and 42 angulis form one kishtu. 2000 dhanus are called one gavyuti. 4 gavyuti form one yojana which equals 8000 dhanus.

A dwelling house is called a shala and a palace is called a prasada.

In treta yuga Brahma ordained varnashrama dharmas or observance of caste system.

This purana also narrates the Vishnu avataras of Matsya, Narasimha, Vamana, Dattatreya, Bhavya, Parasurama, Rama, Vedavyasa, Krishna and Kalki. The virtues and the holiness of Gaya are discussed.

Varaha purana: Prithvi (earth) was kept in captivity by demon Hiranyaksha in 'Rasatala'. Narayan kills and brings back the earth to its proper position. As in other puranas the tale of creation is narrated. The ten incarnations of Lord Vishnu were mentioned. The tales of Dharmavyadha, Gaurmukha, Agastya and Daksha were narrated. Priyavrata's going to Heaven, Ashwasira's liberation, the emancipation of king Vasu, sage Raimya, and the story of Durjay form part of this purana. Pitris and the importance of Shradh and the details of its performance were included in this purana. Agni, Ashwinikumars, goddess Parvati, Lord Ganapathi, Kartikeya, and Aditya are the divine personalities about whom information is presented. In order to kill Andhakasur, a demon, the creation of 'Ashtamatrikas' was explained. The combined powers of the deities namely, Vaishnavi from Vishnu, Brahmi from Brahma, Varahi from Varah, Maheswari from Narayana, Yogeswri from Shiva, Kaumari from Kartikeya, Mahendri from Indra and Yami from Yama constitute the eight mothers Dharma was created from the right part of the Almighty to protect mankind from evil and sin. Tarpan given to pitris on new moon day liberates from sin. A number of vratas or rituals performed on specific days of the year bestow specific benefits to the performer. These sre :

Matsya dvadasi vrata on the 12 day of Margasira,

Kurma dvadasi vrata on the 12 day of Pausha,

Varaha dvadsi vrata on the 12 day of Magh,

Narasimha dvadasi vrata on the 12 day of Phalgun,

Jamadagnya dvadasi vrata on the 12 day of Vaisakh,

Kalki dvadasi vrata on the 12 day of Bhadrapad,

Padmanabh dvadasi vrata on the 12 day of Aswin,

Dharani dvasasi vrata on the 12 day of Kartik,

Sri Krishna dvadasi vrata on the 12 day of Ashadh,

Budha dvadasi vrata on the 12 day of Shravan and

Subh vrata on the first day of Margasirsh.

In addition several rituals to be performed for one year such as Dhanya vrata, Kanti vrata, Saubhagya vrata, Avighna vrata, kaam vrata, Arogya vrata, Putraprapti vrata, Shaurya and Sarvabhouma vrata as well as various rituals connected with sacrificing gifts are narrated. Several holy places were described including Hardwar (Mayapuri), Hrushikesh (Kubjaamrak), Badarika Mandir, Somanath Linga, Salagram Kshetra, Kurukshetra, Gonishkraman kshetra and Dwaraka. Further places where holy dip in waters can be taken so that liberation from sins can be attained called Tirthas, such as Gokarna, Govarthan, Kapil, Chakra, and Lohargal, were highlighted. Mathura, the birth place of Lord Krishna is described. The procedure for installing deities made of wood, stone, earthen and copper, silver and gold are elaborated. Rituals performing the last rites are described. The virtues of maintaing chastity were briefed. The means for realization of Lord Vishnu were introduced. The inseparable relationship between Prakruti and Purush (nature and man or god) was eulogized. On the geography side the various dwipas or islands called Jambu dwipa, Shak dwipa, Kush dwipa, Kraunch dwipa and Shalmali dwipa were described. The existence of Himalayas, Sumeru, Hemakut and Nishad mountains on the four sides of Jambudwip was discussed. The killing of Mahishasura by Shakti is also the subject matter of this purana.

Vishnu purana: Sage Parasara told rishi Maitreya about the creation of the universe in this purana. At the time of the creation, the present world was all full of water. From the waters emerged a huge egg, called Brahmanda in which the whole universe was contained. It was surrouned by water, air, fire and sky. Vishnu as Brahma creates the world and as Shiva destroys it. When the earlier creation was destroyed there was only water and Vishnu slept on water and hence was called Narayana. He became a boar and brought the earth from underneath the water. The earth was divided into seven regions. Brahama, part of Narayana, created Asuras, Demons, deities or gods, pitris or ancestors, and then the humans and many other beings. Yakshas wanted to eat Brahma as they were hungry and Rakshasas tried to protect him. The horrified Brahma created snakes from his hairs. Gandharvas were born then. Birds, goats, sheep, cattle, horses, elephants, deers, camels were also born from Him. Plants sprouted from his hairs. Men of all the four caste men were born.

Once sage Durvasa got angry with Indra the chief of devas and cursed him. All the gods became weak. Vishnu advised the deities to churn the sea with the assistance of demons. During the churning process Lakshmi was born. She granted several boons to devas or deities. The story of Manu, Priyavrata, Uttanapada and Dhruva appear in this purana also. The story of Vena, the bad king and the birth of Prithu was narrated. One of the descendents was Prachinavarhi. This his wife Savarna bore him ten children called Prachetas. They were all married to Marisha. Daksha was born to Marisha. Daksha had sixty daughters. Kashyap married thirteen of them. To his son Hiranyakaship, Prahlad along with three others Anuhlada, Hlada and Sunhlada were born. The story of Prahlada a great devotee of Vishnu is well known.

Priyavrata had ten sons. One of his sons Agnidhra got Jambudvipa to share to his kingdom. He had nine sons and divided his kingdom Jambudvipa and distributed the various parts to them to rule. One part went to his son Rishabha and later to his grandson Bharata. That part was called after his grandson Bharatavarsha. It may be once again mentioned that the seven dvipas which constituted earth were called Jambudvipa Shalmalidvipa, Krounchadvipa, Palkshadvipa, Shakadvipa, Pushkaradvipa and Kushadvipa. These seven dvipas were surrounded by seven oceans called, Lavana (salt), Ikshu (sweet), Dadhi (curd), Dughdha (milk), Jala (fresh water), Sura (alcohol), and Sarpi. Jambudvipa was at the center. Middle of that was Meru, the famous mountain.

The sacred river Ganga is described. Jambudvipa was surrounded by Lavana ocean (sea of salt). Bharatavarsha is the best part of Jambudvipa.

Seven under worlds were mentioned They are Atala, Vitala, Nitala, Gabhastimala, Mahatala, Sutala and Patala. Yakshas, Nagas, Danavas and Daityas live in these worlds. A description of Hell, the kingdom of Yama is given.

Dhruva is the center of all the stars. The worlds above are Janalok, Tapolok and Satylok which was divided into Brahmalok and Vaikunthlok further. The story of Jadabharata, who was attached to a deer and had to take therefore several more births before emancipation is also narrated. Attachment leads to miseries and renunciation or detachment assists in liberation.

According to this purana seven manvantaras were completed and seven more are to go before dissolution of the universe. The sage who divided the Vedas for this age was Krishna Dwaipayana. Vedas were divided in the past 28 times. The next Vyasa will be Aswatthama the son of Dronacharya of Mahabharata fame. Sage Vaisampayana divided Yajurveda into 27 parts and distributed among his disciples. Due to some problem one of his disciples Yajnavalkya had to return the Veda learnt from Vaisampayana. This is called Taittareya Sakha or branch. Committed to learn Yajurveda Yajnavalkya did a great penance and obtained Yajurvedic hymns from the sun god Surya. This part of Veda is called Shukla or white Yajurveda. Surya taught him in the form of a horse or Vaji. The purana further explains the four classes of people or four castes and also the four ashramas or stages of life. The rituals to be observed are also explained.

Some dynasties from Manu onwards are detailed. The stories of Ikshvaku, Yuvanahva, Saubhari, Mandhata, King Sagara and his Aswamedha, Bhagiratha, Saudasa and Vasishta and Nimi, the son of Ikshvaku, are narrated.

On the side of lunar dynasties the birth of Budha to Tara and Chandra (moon) was included. Satyavati and Richaka had a son Jamadagni. To Jamadagni and Renuka, Parasurama was born. He was an incarnation of Lord Vishnu. The stories of Nahusha, Yayati, Shyamantaka jewel and Krishna, Shishupala, Shantanu who married Ganga were all retold in this purana also. In the age of Kali the dynasty of Mahapadmananda , a shudra ruled for 100 years Bharat varsha. With the help of Kautilya, a Brahmin, Mouryas ruled for 137 years. Shunga dynasty ruled for 112 years. Kanva kings ruled for 45 years. Andhras ruled for 456 years. Later several outsiders entered the country and ruled this country. This Kali yuga lasts 3,60, 000 years . People suffer during the Kali age.

The story of Vasudeva and Devaki the parents of Krishna and the related events were narrated. Kamsa, Putana, Kaliya the snake king, Dhenukasura, Pralambasura, the lifting of Govardhan mountain, and several other exploits of Krishna were narrated. The killing of Kamsa and Jarasanda was also included. The story of Kalayavana was explained. Marriage of Krishna with Rukmini, Narakasura's killing, the story of Parijatha, Usha and Banasura, the slaying of Poundraka Vasudeva are the other topics included. The wedding of Samba, the son of Krishna was another highlight. The end of the Yadava dynasty too was described. All these and other stories of the purana suggest to men the ways to attain salvation or mukti.

CHAPTER 15

The Agamas

Sruti is considered to be of two forms; Nigama and Agama. Nigama or Veda is authority. Agama is advice based on vedic authority. Agamas are the theological treatises and manuals for divine worship. They utilize many vedic verses (mantras). They lay down the procedures for external worship of God. They contain temple building, idol making or iconometry, devotion, meditation methods for liberation, yoga, philosophy of mantras, mystic diagrams, charms, spells, domestic practices, civil codes, social observances, public festivals and others. In fact it can be said that agamas revolve around mantras (sound energy), yantras (contrivances charged with the energy of mantra), and tantra an elaborate procedure that puts mantra to specific use for the practitioner. All the vedic hymns are mantras only. Yantra and tantra will be briefly explained.

Yantra: Yantra could be a geometrical figure as in a devata yantra (Sreeyantra, for example) or it could be an instrument as in an astra (weapon). Each devata has a yantra that represents the nature of the energy associated with that devata. The yantra could be a figure or shape drawn on the floor using turmeric or could be an engraved figure on a metallic plate. These figures are worshipped and charged with the energy of the corresponding mantra.

Tantra: Tantra is a method with philosophy contained in it. There are three forms of tantra, namely, Dakshina, Vama and Madhyama corresponding to satvic, rajasic and tamasic attributes of tantra respectively.

Dakshina practice involves mind and mental attitude. Vama practices involve physical codes and actions to vitalize the energy centers in the body. Thus, all tantra practices serve the practitioners to activate and use energy for specific purposes.

There are three agamas, namely

(a) The Vaishnava agamas, wherein Lord Vishnu is glorified.

(b) The Shaiva agamas which glorify Shiva as the Supreme God and

(c) The Shakta agamas that worship mother nature or mother universe as Devi.

Each agama contains four aspects: Jnana (knowledge), Yoga (meditation methods), Kriya (rituals) and Charya (moral codes etc.).

There are several Vaishnava agamas of which Pancharatra, Vaikhanasa, Pratishtasara and Vijnana Lalita agamas are more prominent. Some others are Iswara, Ahirbhudhnya, Narada, Paushkara, Satvata Jnanamritasara etc. It is said that there are about 200 to 225 Vaishnava agama texts. On the Shaiva agamas side there are 28 agamas. Sixty four Sakta agamas are identified and there could be even more. All the agamas are not derived from Vedas but are vedic in spirit and character as mentioned earlier. The agamas teach several occult practices also.

The Vaishnava agamas: In these agamas Vishnu is the main Godhead. Pancharatra agamas contain five fold ritual schedule. Here Lord Vishnu is said to manifest in Para, Vyuha, Vibhava, Antaryami and Archa forms. The formless Absolute Transcendent 'Parabrahma' is brought into the mundane world for worship in a manifest form.

Para is the immanent manifestation of the Supreme Being.

Vyuha manifestation refers to successive transcendence of the Divine to the jeeva level.

Vasudeva is the first level with six characteristics which are equally shared by the successive manifestations.

Samkarshana is the second level manifestation with jnana (knowledge) and bala (strength) attributes.

Pradyumna is the third level manifestation with aiswarya (wealth) and virya (power).

Aniruddha is the final manifestation in the lotus of the heart as jeevatma with shakti (energy), and tejas (brilliance). The Supreme Being (Para) is unaffected by vyuhas or the various emanations.

Vibhava: This is the explanation for 'avatara' or incarnation. The Divine power descends from the vyuha deities as an avatara. The Supreme is unaffected.

Antaryamin manifestation: This is Aniruddha who as jeevatma is located in the hearts of all the beings that are created. He is the mysterious power that is the inner self of all the souls.

Archa manifestation: An idol of Vishnu is consecrated as per the rites of Panchratra. It acquires power from Vishnu. The idol is meant for daily worship. This is not to be confused with worshipping replica or model of god for concentrating on the Absolute. In this case once concentration is achieved the model or pratima is no more needed and can be dispensed with.

The essence of Vaishnava worship consists of the following.

- keeping oneself under God's care.
- Humility and knowledge of one's own ignorance and deficiencies.
- Unshakable faith in God, Narayana.
- Accepting Narayana as the sole protector.
- Giving up antagonism to any of the God's creation.
- Doing good to all beings.

The Saiva agamas: In these agamas Lord Shiva is the supreme Godhead. The 28 Saiva agamas are divided into two classes. Ten belong to Sivabheda and the rest eighteen belong to Rudrabheda agamas. Another demarcation puts them under four classes : Kapala, Kalamukha, Pasupata and Saiva. Kashmira Saiva is popular in northern India, while, Siddhanta saiva is practiced in southern India. Kamika, Vira, Parameswara and Swayambhuva are some of the saiva agamas. These agamas contain trillions of verses. For example, Kamika agama contains 100,000,000,000,000,0000 (denoted by parartha) verses. Sukshma agama contains 100,000,000,000,0000 (denoted by padma) verses or slokas. It is believed that the Saiva agamas originated from the five faces Sadyojata, Vamadeva, Aghora, Tatpurusha and Eeshana of Lord Shiva. There are 204 upaagamas supporting the Saiva agmas. All these agamas have four parts : Charya (atonement), Kriya (puja or japa or homa or rites), Yoga (36 procedures or tattvas and Jnana (explanation of pashu, pathi and pasha).

The Sakta Agamas: Some scholars classify tantras as belonging to Sakta agamas. Sakti (energy) is worshipped as mother of the universe. Numerous methods of ritualistic worship of the Divine Mother are mentioned in the literature. These agamas are in the form of a dialogue between Parvati and Shiva. The queries raised by Shiva are answered by Parvati as the Divine Mother. These Sakta agamas are of two kinds: Vama and Dakshina. While 64 agamas are identified as of now there could be even more of them not brought to light. Some of the prominent agamas are Kularnava, Rudra yamala, Brahma yamala. Vishnu yamala, Mahanirvana etc. Certain extreme practices of vamachara are against the vedic spirit. Eating meat, sexual union and drinking alcohol, living with corpses are not in accordance with Vedas. Adi Sankara has expelled many of such practices and reformed Hinduism.

Mantra

Mantra is the power of sound. Even though it appears that there is a relation between the sound and the meaning of the sound uttered, in fact, no such relation exists. The effect of a mantra is dependent on the various qualities of sounds made such as decibel level its melody, decibel level, variations in the pitch, shortening or lengthening of a syllable in a composite word and others. The great rishis who observed the power of sounds and words had meditated upon these words and created mantras. These specified sounds constitute seed letters (Beejakshara). Uttering these mantras, meditating upon them and observing the places from where the sounds of the seed letters are being created leads one to attain the power of the mantra. This requires absolute concentration on mantra.

In any mantra the seed letters are arranged in a specific form by the rishis. When the mantra is uttered with intense devotion they create a new awareness that was not present earlier in the meditator. The power of the mantra gets invoked at the respective power centers in the body when regularly meditated with absolute devotion.

Mantras may contain one, two or more words. They may even be a 'stotra' (a long prayer with verses). Each prayer has a specific result. AUM is the most important mantra that contains the three aspects of creation, sustenance and dissolution. Its extention is Gayatri. In subtle form it is "SOHAM" and in full form it is the eight worded Gayatri mantra. The importance of mantras in yogic life can not be described in words but must be experienced.

CHAPTER 16

Tantra

Literally tantra means knitting in Sanskrit. The science of tantra belongs to Yajurveda. The Divine Consciousness is manifesting in human body as Self. The art and science of realizing this Self is dealt in tantra. Tantra is a technique through which one can realize the Divine nature in the body and the effulgence of embodied soul, called "Jeevatma". The technique of understanding the soul or spirit in the body is also called Brahmavidya. Tantra deals with the various physical aspects that pertain to self realization.

This science is based on the existence of certain centers of power or energy in the human body called 'Chakras' or Plexuses. According to Hindu scriptures the whole universe is supported by a big serpent. So also, according to tantra the basic or static energy in the human body is coiled up at a point below the navel. This creative force, the primal cosmic energy in the body is called Kundalini, and is outside the electromagnetic energy spectrum. It is lying there dormant in a coiled up form like a snake. Hence, it is called snake power or kundalini. The technique of arousing this dormant kundalini in the body is practiced as kundaliniyoga, layayoga or chakrabedha yoga. It is metaphysically, scientifically and para psychically of great interest. Its existence was noticed and experienced by Indian spiritual masters of yoga called yogis well over 5000 years.

The following explains the parallelism between human anatomy and yogic energy pathways and centers. We all know that human body is made up of cells. "To maintain the functioning of the cells, tissues and the whole system of human body at its optimum level in its internal environment a sort of uniformity has to be maintained. Physically, the body temperature is maintained constant. In the same way chemically the pH value is maintained constant. This necessitated the body to possess a biological control system. Thus, there are two control systems provided:

1. The nervous system and
2. The endocrinal system.

The basic structural and functional unit of the nervous system is the neuron. Each neuron is made up of a nerve cell. A nerve cell has a central nucleus around which is a cell body. From this nerve body nerve fibers called dendrites of shorter lengths and one of longer length called axon arise. Dendrites conduct all impulses from the periphery to the nerve cell. The axons carry the impulses away from the cell.

The central nervous system consists of brain and spinal cord. In this system all the nerve cells are grouped together in the cortical grey matter of the brain and the central grey matter of the spinal cord and the various nuclei of the peripheral nervous system that are located in ganglia. The nerve fibers are grouped together to form tracts of central nervous system and the peripheral nerves.

The peripheral nervous system contains sensory and motor nerves. The spinal cord has five distinct parts.

The lowest part in the coccygeal region has three vertebrae that are fused as a single bone. This is called coccyx. In the sacral region above the coccyx there are five fused vertebrae called sacrum. Above the sacrum in the lumbar region five vertebrae are present. The spinal cord contains in the dorsal region (back side) twelve vertebrae. Lastly in the cervical region there are seven vertebrae. The total vertebrae are 33 in number.

The spinal nerves after their exit from the inter vertebral foramina enter into communication with the gangliated cords of sympathetic nervous system, that lies on either side of the vertebral column. In the case of humans as we know, the spinal cord exits from the upper boarder of atlas below the cerebellum and passes through medulla. It finally opens into the fourth ventricle of the brain. It descends to lumbar vertebrae where it tapers to a point called filam terminale. Here a highly sensitive grey matter exists. This is the position where the coiled up serpent power kundalini is said to exist and this location is identified with an energy center called Muladhara. These energy centers are explained now.

Yoga deals with chakras which are centers of energy and nadis which are subtle lines of direction along which vital forces travel in the body.

In the science of tantra there are basically seven chakras identified, of which six are inside the body.

They are Muladhara at coccygeal, Svadhishtan at sacral region, Manipura at lumbar region, Anahata at dorsal region, and Visudha at cervical region respectively. The sixth energy center in the body is located between the two eye brows and is called Ajna chakra. All these chakras are in the space. Slightly above the center of the head the seventh chakra 'Sahasrara' or Crown chakra is located.

"The chakras are concerned with the central or spinal nervous system comprising the brain or encephalon in the skull and the spinal cord, also called Merudanda. On either side of the vertebral column there is a chain of ganglia connected with nerve fiber called sympathetic cord. This is identified as Ida and Pingala in tantric nadi system, existing on either side of merudanda. These two nadis will be considered again, later. This sympathetic cord extends all the way from the base of the skull to the coccyx in communication with the spinal cord".

In the region of Visudha, Anahata, and Manipura where lungs, heart and stomach are located the existence of ganglia corresponding to spinal nerves is noteworthy.

It has been pointed out earlier that the positions of Visudha, Anahata, Manipura, Svadhishtan and Muladhara correspond to the five parts of the vertebral column mentioned. They are now related to the various plexuses in the body.

- Muladhra --- Sacral plexus
- Svadhishtan --- Prostatic plexus.
- Manipura --- Solar plexus.
- Anahata --- Cardiac plex
- Visudha --- Laryngeal plexus.
- Ajna --- Cavernous plexus

Even though Sahasrara is not located in the body it is related to cerebellum which is called 'Mount Kailasa' in yogic and spiritual sense.

Chakras which are centres for expression of consciousness are also related through intermediate conductors with the gross organs of generation, digestion, cardiac action and respiration.

In the tantric system nadis are the conduits for prana or vital force. These tantric nerves or nadis are large in number. The word nadi is derived from "nad" or motion. In the body the life force moves along the nadis. It is generally believed that there are 72,000 nadis in the body. Some are gross and correspond to arteries and veins. Some others are very subtle and are called yoga nadis. Of these only 14 nadis are considered as principal nadis. Among these nadis again, three nadis are considered most important and are called Ida, Pingala and Sushumna.

Sushumna is the greatest nadi to which all others are subordinate. On the left side of Sushumna, Ida or moon nadi and on the right side Pingala, the sun nadi are present. Inside the Sushumna, another nadi Vajrini is present. The power that flows through Vajrini is called chitrini. Sushumna is located in the interior of cerebro spinal axis or merudanda. Sushumna nadi is said to possess tamasic guna (quality) and is red in colour. Vajrini is rajasic and lustrous as it is like electric current. Chitrini is satvic in character and represents divine consciouness. The two nadis Ida and

Pingala alternate from right to left and from left to right around the six chakras. Muladhara chakra is the meeting place for these two with Sushumna and hence that place is called Yukta Triveni meaning confluence of three. After their travel around the chakras, they reach the space between the two eye brows. Here they enter the Sushumna and make a plaited knot of the three and hence is called Mukta Triveni. They separate out there after at Ajna chakra. Ida moves into left eye brow and Pingala enters right eye brow.

Now the various chakras will be explained:

Muladhara Chakra

This energy center is at the mouth of Sushumna placed below the genitals and above the anus. In other words it is at the base of the spinal column. Spiritually this chakra is the seat where matter, life energy and soul are blended harmoniously for the development of the physical body. Here kundalini sleeps in snake like form as mentioned earlier in three and half coils. This formation is explained in various ways. The first coil represents the dormant state in evolution. Such a state exists in minerals and inanimate forms. The second coil stands for the dream state experienced by plants and trees where vital pulsations are awake, and such physical activities that are necessary for growth and survival like respiration, acceptance of food, flowering, fructification etc., take place. The third coil signifies an awakened state with senses working in addition to physical activities that take place in plants. This is a state where the mind is still not fully developed. Animals live in this state. They know how to consume food and do not know to give to others. They have no thinking capacity beyond a level. The half coil with raised hood represents the completely awakened state of mind that exists in humans. This is symbolized by the raised hood of the snake. Another way of interpreting serpent symbol is to identify the three coils with physical matter, life force and soul as stated before. The raised hood of the half coil denotes the awakened consciousness. Muladhara takes the responsibility of creation or formation through cell or molecular division in minerals and plants

The consciousness at Muladhara is in 'supta' or dormant state. This corresponds to the earlier statement that kundalini is tamasic and hence needs to be aroused into action. Physically this means that cells and tissues are produced here. Muladhara chakra is responsible for proper generation and functioning of muscular and bone system. It keeps a balance between salts and other chemicals in the in the body. If this chakra is not properly developed arthritis, spinal cord disorders, loss of energy, loss of growth, leukemia, bone cancer and allergies etc., may result and afflict the body. In aged persons this chakra becomes weak.

The nervous system leaves the spine running down both the legs like a massive root system called sciatic nerve. This is the largest peripheral nervous system in human body. It leaves sacral plexus and spreads down to feet and toes. It provides a direct path to mother earth. Thus, as it provides a physical support to the body Muladhara chakra is also called base chakra and also root chakra. Further human body is a magnet and this chakra is the south pole of this magnet while the head is the north pole of the body magnet.

Svadhishtan Chakra

This chakra is some times called spleenic chakra. Hara is another name for this energy center. This chakra is located slightly below the navel area. Its main function is to manifest primal creative energy into functional sexual energy. Svadhishtan is responsible for reproduction in animals and in humans through union.

For this reason this chakra is also called sexual chakra. This is considered as a seat for feelings and emotions. This chakra has control over brain tissue. Mal functioning of this chakra may lead to diseases related to uterus and reproductive system.

Manipura Chakra

It is generally called solar plexus. It is located slightly above the navel. It is a very complex energy center. Organizational skills and personal power are the qualities associated with this chakra. This chakra has control over small intestine, large intestine, gall bladder, liver and appendix and if this center does not function properly problems associated with intestines may arise. Loss of vigor and appendicitis may also result. It has profound control over liver.

Anahata Chakra

This chakra is located in the middle of the chest. It is on the spinal cord right opposite to the heart. This chakra is associated with love and compassion. This energy center controls heart, lungs, blood circulating system and also liver. This chakra helps produce blood in the body. If this chakra does not function properly anaemia may result.

It controls thymus gland. Malfunctioning of this chakra may result in T.B, asthma , and lung related diseases as well as skin related disorders.

Body equilibrium is maintained by Anahata and Manipura chakras

Visudha Chakra

This chakra is also called throat chakra as this chakra is located at the throat on the spinal column. By virtue of its location it controls the communication system in the body which is larynx. This chakra has great influence on thyroid and para thyroid glands. Both tongue and ears are under its influence.

If this chakra becomes weak diseases affecting nose, throat, ears and mouth may manifest.

Ajna Chakra

The chakras so far discussed are below the head and are associated with energies of lower frequencies. This sixth chakra is related to autonomous nervous system, hypothalamus. It controls the pituitary gland. It is the seat of will power and intuition. And is located between the two eye brows. Eyes and nose are directly controlled by this chakra. This chakra controls all the chakras discussed earlier and deals with energies of higher frequencies. Ajna chakra controls bone marrow and hence influences blood production, especially the red corpuscles. A weak Ajna chakra causes anaemia.

There are moods in the mind. These moods work at all the energy centers mentioned so far. There are no moods working at Sahasrara. These moods are distributed among the chakras. Further, there are three yogic glands working in the body. The six chakras are paired into three groups in order and are influenced by these glands. This is given below in a table

The 360 moods or rays also represent the measure of time as the number of days in a year as well as the total number of rays or angles that emanate from a point in space. Brahma Grandhi is related to creation and related matters. Vishnu Grandhi is related to aspects connected with maintenance of the body in good health. Rudra Grandhi indicates will power. Visudha and Ajna chakras enable the mind to think about higher aspects in life destroying the base instincts in humans. Thus, the principle of destruction and dissolution are explained by Rudra. Mind becomes satvic due the awakening of these two chakras or due to Rudra Grandhi.

Chakra	Moods (Kalaas)	Glands
Muladhara	56	Brahma Grandhi
Svadhishtan	62	
Manipura	52	Vshnu Grandhi
Anahata	54	
Visudha	72	Rudra Grandhi
Ajna	64	
Total	360	

(See 'Soundarya Lahari' verse 14 by Shri Adi Shankaracharya)

Sahasrara Chakra

This chakra is also called crown chakra. It is located right on the top of the head. It is a swirling energy vortex associated with pineal gland. It controls brain and connects us to the spiritual self. Here the individual consciousness merges with the universal consciousness. Awakening of this chakra leads to annihilation of the existence of the Self. This is 'Self realization'.

The Universal Life Force which is described as white in color gets dispersed into its constituent colors of violet, indigo, blue, green, yellow, orange and red at the seven chakras, namely, Sahasrara, Ajna, Visudha, Anahata, Manipura, Svadhishtan and Muladhara respectively.

Petals: At each of these energy centres, tantra identifies a lotus with definite number of petals. These lotuses are arranged one above the other from Muladhara to Sahasrara

At Muladhara the lotus has 4 petals and at Svadhishtan 6 petals. The lotus at Manipura has 10 petals and the lotus at Anahata 12 petals. At Visudha and Ajna centres there are 16 and 2 petals respectively .

These petals correspond to the sounds produced by the 50 alphabetic letters of Sanskrit, the language of Gods. When all the chakras are well developed then these sounds can be well pronounced. The following shows the correspondence of the various centers to the petals or letters.

Plexus	Petals	Letters
Muladhara	4	Va, Sa, Shaw, Sah
Svadhishtan	6	Ba, Bha, Ma, Ya, Ra, La
Manipura	10	Da, Dha, Nna, Ta, Tha, Da, Ddha, Na, Pa, Pha
Anahata	12	Ka, Kha, Ga, Gha, Jna, Cha Chha, Ja, Jha, Gna, Ta, Tha
Visudha	16	A, AA, I, Ie, u, uu, Ru, Roo, Lu, Loo, E, Ai, O, Au, Am, Aha
Ajna	2	Ha, Ksha

Muladhara Chakra is considered as a lotus of **four** petals symbolizing seed, place, water and time the most needed for creation of life form. Seed is the semen of the male. Place is the abdomen of the female. Water is the liquids in the stomach of the mother that nourishes the embryo. Finally, time is the appropriate time that is congenial for pregnancy and then for growth and delivery of the child. At the global level, the creation of minerals and others takes place at the south pole. At the solar level this power comes from the planet Saturn. Mooladhara corresponds to earth related features. The power at this chakra is called "**Dhakini**". The four letters are also identified as the four directions along which the creation expanded. They also represent the four Vedas. Mooladhara is the centre for production of atoms, cells, tissues and the other needed materials. The divine spirit is lying here in a dormant state or sleep state (Supta). At the universal level the star Moola of Sagittarius sign of the zodiac is the mooladhara. Creation of atoms, minerals, solar systems from the great (para Sakti) energy of the universe is under the control of this star moola. This is desribed as "Fohat digging holes in space" by Mrs Blavetsky in her book 'Secret Doctrine'. This means that out of the unmanifest, the manifestation of solar systems take place.

Svadhishtan is the centre for the birth of beings, formation of mind and organs. The **six** letters here are the five sense organs and the mind. (cf. Shaadgunya paripoorita – Lalita sahasranama). This centre is near spleen in the human body. It keeps the body temperature at appropriate level. The power at this center is called "**Rakini**". She is said to be seated on 'Makara" or Capricorn (zodiac sign). When sun enters Capricorn the layers of ice are removed and earth warms up. Sun light restores life force (prana). When sun enters Cancer or Karkataka sign it rains and plant kingdom starts its life cycle once again. Again when the 'Makara' is in the west, Karkataka will be in the east. Then Mesha (Aries) will be just over the head. On the eighth day of the lunar fortnight (Ashtami) when the sun sets in the west in "Makara', 'Karkataka', will be rising in the east while Aries will be just overhead. On that day the moon will be of half his size. There will be light and darkness evenly distributed. Light indicates God and darkness indicates creation. For one who looks at both of them evenly, there will be moonlight and no darkness. Moonlight symbolizes consciousness of the mind, derived from solar consciousness which in turn comes from cosmic consciousness from space (primordeal ocean). Rakini is responsible for inducing sleep state so that the body regains energy.

Manipura chakra contains **ten** letters or petals. They stand for aversion, fear, infatuation, sorrowful state, deep sleep, desire, jealousy, inferiority, excitement and shame. This chakra establishes balance of liquids in the body. This chakra is near navel. There is inherent energy in the form of 'vaisvanaragni' in water. It contains matter, energy and consciousness. It is responsible for the evolution of life. The energy presiding this chakra is called '**Lakini**'. In the universe this power is responsible for the rotation of earth around the sun so that day, night and seasons are formed. Atmosphere is created around the earth. Life could thereby exist on this planet.

Anahata is located near the heart. It is in a region of air (Vayu). The lotus here has **twelve** petals that represent the 12 months in the year. They are also related to the 12 signs of the zodiac. Each sign rules an organ in human body. Aries rules the head, Taurus the face, Jamini the neck and the hands, Cancer the chest, Leo the heart, Virgo the stomach, Libra the navel, Scorpion the reproductory organs, Sagittarius the lower spinal region,and Pisces the feet. The presiding deity of this chakra is called 'Kakini'. The respiratory process is under its control.

Visudha chakra located at the throat has 16 petals representing the sixteen phases of the moon. The energy centre is identifid as a deity called '**Sakini**'. She has the power to produce sounds and join them as words with meaning.

Ajna chakra exists at the middle of the **two** eye brows. It is near two endocrine glands, pineal and pituitary. In terms of jyotish (astrology and astronomy) these two glands are the zodiac sign Pisces. In the secret interpretation of jyotish, after Sagittarius the zodiac moves upward with Pisces ending in the head. In the general approach Pisces is identified with the feet. There is an interrelationship between feet and the glands in the head. Touching the feet of Jnanis' (enlightened persons) awakens the Ajna chakra of the worshipper. Ajna chakra has controlling power on bone marrow. The power at Ajna chakra is called '**Hakini**'.

Sahasrara has the attributes of all the sounds or letters and is thus addressed as sarvavarnatmika. This is above 'sushumna' nadi. The divine power at this center is called '**Yakini**'.

Above 'Visudha' and below 'Ajna' there is a subtle chakra or energy center called "Lalana". Further, between 'Sahasrara' and 'Ajna' there is another subtle chakra called 'Mahasunya'. These nine energy centers are explained as the nine enclosures in "Srichakra".

At each of the seven energy centers tantra identifies a specific male and female power as the presiding deities. This is how tantra sastra brings natural forces in the universe through sounds and in concept as gods and goddesses into human body.

CHAPTER 17

Gita

The Essence of Vedic Philosophy

In Gita Lord Krishna addressed the humanity through Arjuna and explained the essence of philosophy when Arjuna the Pandava prince faced the dilemma of fighting against his own close relatives and teachers and entered a state of great depression.

The soul in the body passes into another body just as it passes through childhood, youth and old age after death. Wise men do not weep neither for the dead nor for the living. The soul (Atma) is eternal, imperishable and incomprehensible. The immutable soul can never be destroyed. It is unborn, eternal permanent and primeval. Whatever is born is destined to die and whatever dies will born again.

Pleasure and pain, gain and loss, victory and defeat are to be treated alike. Man is entitled only to work and not to its fruit. Working with an even mind giving up all attachment, treating success and failure alike is called yoga. Yoga is also defined as skill in action. One should not get perturbed by adversity and should not rejoice in prosperity.

If one dwells on his mind and the objectives of sense, an attachment develops in his mind. Attachment gives rise to desire. Desire breeds anger. From anger comes delusion which leads to loss of recollection. Loss of recollection leads to loss of comprehending capacity. Then one perishes with lack of understanding.

Through keeping senses under full control, giving up both love and hatred, clear vision can be obtained. This ends all sorrow. The secret to attain peace is giving up the feeling of "I" and "mine". Then a divine state is attained.

This is the yoga of knowledge or **Sankhya yoga**

In the yoga of works or **'Karma yoga',** the Lord prescribed for men of contemplation the path of knowledge and for men of action the path of work (Karma).

No man can remain idle. Everyone does some work. Man is driven to work by the impulses of nature. One should control his senses along with mind and then direct his organs of action to work without attachment. All work should be done as a sacrifice.

From food all creatures are born; from rain food is produced; and from sacrifice comes rain. Thus, sacrifice is the root for the existence of life.

Work without attachment is supreme. All work is done by the disposition of nature. But, man is deluded by the feeling of self and thinks that he is the doer.

It is the organs of sense that are occupied with the objects of sense. Those who are misled by the disposition of nature are attached to the works which those dispositions prompt.

Love and hatred are bound to arise towards the objects of each sense. They are one's enemies. It is always better to follow one's own conscience rather than follow other's law.

True knowledge is enveloped by insatiable fire of desire which springs from passion. Desire is the foe of the wise.

The senses, the mind and the understanding are the seat of desire. Through them it veils the knowledge and deludes the soul.

In the yoga of divine knowledge, or **'Jnana yoga'** the Lord conveyed that for protection of the good, for destruction of the wicked and for the establishment of the law, He is born from time to time.

One can reach Him by giving up passion, fear and anger. One should totally surrender himself unto the Lord, seeking refuge in Him and be completely absorbed in His thought.

The concept of work is explained by the Lord. He who sees no work in work and work in no work is a wise person or yogi. The person whose works are burnt up by the fire of knowledge is a sage.

One who gives up attachment to the fruit of works, and is always satisfied – is never engaged in work. He does no work at all eventhough he may engage himself in any avocation.

A person who is always satisfied with whatever he gets, who rises above both pleasure and pain, having no ill will towards any one and who remains the same in success and failure is not bound by the results of the works he does. Such a person is freed from attachments and establishing his mind in knowledge, performs all works as a sacrifice. He realizes God in his works and reaches Him.

There are many kinds of sacrifices. Sacrifice of knowledge is the most glorious one. All works culminate in knowledge and sacrifice of knowledge is thus the greatest sacrifice. Divine knowledge purifies a man. A perfect yogi finds this in himself in course of time.

In the yoga of renunciation of works or '**Sanyasa yoga**' Lord Krishna said that the renunciation of works and their selfless performance both lead to bliss. The spirit of renunciation is explained as possession of neither hatred nor desire. The place reached by men of renunciation is also reached by men of action.

All actions such as "seeing, hearing, touching, smelling, tasting, walking, breathing, speaking" etc., are all performed by the organs. One should feel that all these actions are not performed by him; he should resign all his actions to God. A selfless man who has renounced the fruits of all his actions will attain a disciplined peace of mind. But the man who is not selfless is drawn by desire and is attached to the fruit and is therefore bound.

The freed soul neither works in the world nor causes any one to work. Nor does it connect works with their fruits. It is nature that works. The self realized person, that is, one who has divine knowledge is unattached to external objects, finds happiness within himself – and is in union with God and thus enjoys undying bliss.

Pleasures that arise from attachments are only sources of pain. Resist the force of desire and anger. An important method mercifully gifted to mankind by the Lord to achieve self realization is as follows.

One should shut out all external objects by closing the eyes. The gaze of the eyes is to be fixed between the two eyebrows. The breathing process – that is – the inhalation and exhalation has to be equalized so that slowly the senses are controlled. One has to simultaneously practice giving up completely desire, fear and anger. This process leads to liberation.

In the yoga of meditation or '**Dhyana yoga**' the Lord classified that one who does work with out seeking the fruits of it is a saint (sanyasi) or a yogi. Work is a means to attain yoga but when one attains yoga, serenity is his means.

The spirit of a man who has conquered himself and attained to serenity is steadfast in cold and heat, in pleasure and pain and in honor and dishonor.

A yogi should always try to concentrate his mind in solitude. He should retire to a secret place and control his mind and body. This will enable him get rid of his desires and passions. Sitting on a proper seat, the yogi should practice yoga for his own purification, restraining his thoughts, and senses, bringing his mind to a point. Sitting firm, holding body, head and neck erect and still with steady gaze thinking of the Lord one can attain the eternal bliss. Such a person should observe absolute celibacy.

Once such a state of happiness is reached one is not moved by the heaviest of afflictions. Renouncing entirely, all the desires born of the imagination and restraining with mind all the senses on every side, one can gain tranquility gradually with a steadfast purpose. His mind should concentrates on the Lord thinking of nothing else. A yogi then can see Himself in all beings and all beings in himself. A perfect yogi looks upon all as himself.

In the yoga of experience or **'Jnanavijnana yoga'** the Lord reveals his eight fold division of his nature as earth, water, fire, air, ether, mind, understanding and self consciousness. His higher nature is explained as the immanent spirit that sustains the universe.

The supreme spirit is the origin for all and everything dissolves in Him. He is the taste in waters and light in the sun and the moon. He is in the primal sound AUM. He is the sound in ether. He is the brightness in the fire, and pure fragrance in the earth. He is the life in all creatures. He is in fact the primeval seed.

The three fold disposition of nature – equilibrium, action and inertness or good, passion and dullness arise from Him only. In whatever form one worships the Lord in that form itself he fulfills the desires of his devotees.

In the yoga of imperishable absolute or **'Aksharabrahma yoga'** the Lord explained the imperishable nature of the absolute. As soul He lives in the beings and through works as the creative force He brings beings into existence. All created things are perishable. What ever object one thinks at the time of his death, that object one reaches after his death. At all times, it is required to think of the God.

He who meditates at the time of passing away on the omniscient and primal being, - the Lord, the dispenser of all, who is subtler, whose form is beyond comprehension, who is glorious as the sun, and is beyond all darkness will always reach Him. Closing all the gateways of the body and drawing up the life breath into the head chanting AUM, the single syllable that denotes Brahma, one can reach the supreme while quitting the body.

At the approach of the day of creation all manifest things come forth from an apparent nothingness and at the approach of the night of creation they all merge again into the same nothingness. The state of nothingness is in fact a merged state of all seeds of creation. But beyond this nothingness, there is yet another eternal being, who does not perish when all beings perish. This eternal being is called the 'Imperishable'. Those who reach him will never come back. That is 'Para Brahma'.

In the yoga of sovereign science and sovereign mystery **'Rajavidyarajaguhya yoga'** the Lord propounded the secret of knowledge and experience. This is to be perceived by direct experience, easy to practice and it is eternal.

The Lord pervades the whole universe. The divine sprit is the source of all beings. All beings abide in Him. Under his guidance nature gives birth to all things – those that move and do not move. He is the father, the mother and the supporter. He is the origin and the dissolution. He is the imperishable seed.

By following the rituals enjoined in the Vedas and performing them persons enjoy the fruits of such works and are subject to death and rebirth. Those who meditate on Him and worship Him go only to Him. Whatsoever is done, whatsoever is eaten, whatsoever is offered, whatsoever is given and whatsoever austerities are practiced – shall all be done, so as to be an offering to the Lord – so that the doer can reach the Lord.

In the yoga of manifestation or **'Vibhuti yoga'** the Lord emphasized that he is in fact never understood even by all the gods and sages.

All different attributes such as intelligence, knowledge, sanity, patience, truth, self control, calmness, pleasure and pain, being and non-being, fear and fearlessness, non-violence, equanimity, contentment, austerity, alms giving, fame etc., are all arising out of the Lord's contemplation.

The Supreme spirit, is the origin of all and from him proceed all things. The Lord is the soul seated in the hearts of all creatures. He is the beginning, He is the middle and He is the end. His divine forms are infinite. Wherever power and strength manifest there He is present. Every being that is endowed with grandeur, beauty or strength comes out of the spark of the splendor of the Lord.

In the vision of cosmic form or '**Visvaroopadarsanam**' Lord Krishna revealed his infinite forms which are resplendent, boundless and universal. He declares that he is the mighty world destroying TIME. His cosmic form is accessible only by devotion to Him.

In the yoga of devotion or **'Bhakti yoga'** the Lord advocates that worshipping him with supreme faith will lead to perfect yoga. Knowledge is better than practice of concentration. Meditation is better than knowledge and giving up the fruit of action is even better than meditation, since peace follows it.

Giving up the feeling of "I " and "Mine", remaining contented always, meditating upon the supreme spirit constantly, keeping all the thoughts on

Him are considered to be the qualities of his true devotees. Such a devotion towards Him will lead one to reach Him

In the chapter on distinction between body and the soul or '**Ksetrakshtrajna Vibhaga yoga'**, while distinguishing between body and the soul, the body is explained to consist of self consciousness, understanding and the unmanifested: the ten senses, the mind and the five objects of sense; desire, hatred, pleasure and pain, organism, intelligence and the will to hold together – along with their modifications.

These modifications are – modesty, sincerity, forbearance, uprightness, nonviolence, and many more. The all pervading, all hearing, all seeing and all knowing supreme spirit is without beginning. He is within and with out all beings. He is far away, and yet he is near.

He is undivided and yet He is, as it were, divided among beings. Nature and spirit are both without beginning. All forms and dispositions spring from nature. It is the cause of the formation of the body and its organs. Spirit is the cause of the experience of the pleasure and pain. Spirit seated in nature experiences the disposition of nature. It is the attachments to these dispositions that is the cause of its birth. The Supreme Spirit in the body is the one who witnesses and approves, who supports and enjoys and is the Lord and the Highest self.

In meditation some perceive the spirit in themselves through mind and others by devotion to knowledge and others by devotion to works. When one sees that the manifold nature of beings is centered in the one and that all evolution is only from this one – becomes one with the absolute. The soul is present everywhere and illumines all bodies.

In the fourteenth chapter on differentiation of the three dispositions or '**Gunatraya Vibhaga yoga** the Lord explained the following.

The three dispositions, viz. goodness, passion and dullness or equilibrium, action and inertness arise from nature. They are called Satva, Rajas and Tamas.

Satva is luminous and healthy. It is associated with happiness and the bond of knowledge. Desire is the soul of passion which is the source of thirst and attainment. This binds the soul with the bonds of action. Tamas or inertness is born of ignorance and it deludes all creatures. It binds with negligence, indolence and sleep.

From satvic nature springs knowledge and from passion greed. From tamas springs delusion and ignorance.

The embodied soul must rise above all the three dispositions which the body is made up; then it gains deliverance from birth and death – it becomes immortal. He who is the same in honour and dishonour and the same to friend and foe, the same in pleasure and pain, remains the same amidst pleasant and unpleasant, regards alike both praise and blame and who has renounced all enterprise – has risen above the three dispositions of nature, he reaches the Lord.

In the chapter on the yoga of the Supreme Spirit or '**Purushothama Prapti'**, the imperishable world tree is said to have its roots above and its branches below. The leaves are the Vedas. Its branches extending above and below are nourished by the dispositions of nature. Its twigs are the objects of sense and its clustering roots spread downwards giving rise to actions in the world of men.

One has to cut down the firm rooted tree with strong sword of detachment taking refuge under the primal person praying for his mercy so as to enable the soul to reach him.

Those who are free from pride and delusion, conquering the evil of attachment, abounding desire with absolute devotion to the supreme spirit are sure to reach the abode of peace. They are freed from the pairs of opposites such as pleasure and pain.

The splendor in the sun, moon and fire belongs to the Supreme Spirit. Entering earth he sustains all things by his vital force. Becoming the fire of life he enters into the bodies of all creatures. Mingling with the upward and downward breath He digests food.

He is seated in the hearts of all, and is responsible for memory and knowledge and their loss as well. He is the one to be known by all Vedas and made Vedanta.

There are two beings in this world. The perishable and the imperishable. All the creatures are the perishables, and the imperishable is unchanging. But there is another being, the highest, called the supreme spirit (Parabrahma), who as the eternal Lord pervades and sustains the worlds.

In the distinction between the heritage of the gods and of the demons or '**Daivasura Sampadvibhaga yoga** Bhagavan Sri Krishna gave this message .

Fearlessness, purity of heart, austerity and uprightness, non violence, truth, freedom from anger, renunciation, steadfastness in knowledge and devotion, almsgiving, self control and sacrifice, study of scriptures, tranquility, aversion to slander, compassion to living beings, gentleness, modesty, steadiness, freedom from covetousness, courage, patience and fortitude are the qualities of divine nature in men.

Hypocrisy, arrogance, self conceit, wrath, rudeness, pride and similar qualities are inherent in persons who are of demonic nature. These men of diabolic nature neither know right action nor right abstention. For them, the world is false, without moral basis. They deny the existence of God. They commit cruel deeds. Their actions lead to destruction of the world. Their greed, lust, and wrath are the three gateways for the soul to lose the right path.

The scriptures are the authority in determining the right action. One should work according to scriptural laws.

In threefold division of faith or '**Shradhatraya Vibhaga yoga** Lord Krishna gave the following advice.

The faith of a person depends upon his natural disposition. Worshipping the Lord, teachers, and the wise, purity, uprightness, abstinence and non violence are the penance of the body. Truthful, pleasant and beneficial talk including recitation of Vedas are the penance of the speech. Security of mind, beneficience, silence, self control and purity of heart are the penance of the mind. These three fold penance is practiced with balanced mind by satvic persons or men with "good" dispositions.

Passionate persons or men with "Rajasic" disposition do penance to gain respect, honour and reverence.

Men of "Tamasic" disposition or dull nature perform penance with a foolish obstinacy causing injury to self and others.

In the yoga of renunciation and release or '**Mokshasanyasa yoga**' it is explained that the relinquishing of all works that are prompted by desire is renunciation. Surrendering the fruits of all works is called resignation. Works of sacrifice, gifts and penance purify the wise. They should be done with surrender of attachment and of fruits. Renunciation of any duty that ought to be done is not right.

Knowledge, the object of knowledge and the knowing subject are the three fold incitement to action and the instrument, the purpose and the agent – form the three constituents of action.

Knowledge, action and agent are of three different kinds. Knowledge by which the imperishable is seen in all beings is satvic or "good". Knowledge by which the separateness of things is seen is passionate or "Rajasic". Knowledge by which one understands one and only one object in irrational, untrue and narrow manner is "Tamasic".

An action which is obligatory and is done without love or hatred and without attachment is satvic or good. An action performed with a great strain seeking gratification of desires prompted by "I" ness is "Passionate" or "Rajasic". An action undertaken through ignorance without regard to consequences or to loss and injury is "Tamasic".

The doer who is free from attachment is "Satvic" or good. The doer who is swayed by passion is "Rajasic". The doer who is obstinate, unsteady, malicious, and indolent is "Tamasic". Man reaches perfection by devotion to his own duty. One should do duty that is suited to his nature.

Endowed with a clear vision, firmly restraining himself, turning away from bound and other objects of sense and casting aside likes and dislikes, staying in solitude, eating but little, restraining his speech, body and mind, and engaged in meditation and concentration, cultivating freedom from passions, giving up completely conceit, violence, pride, desire, wrath and possession, self less and tranquil in mind one can become one with God.

CHAPTER 18

Man and Happiness

Mind

Mind is the seat of thoughts. Thoughts arise out of the inherent characteristics of mind that are ever willing, yearning, prompting and insisting on effort and action. Mind contains the impressions or experiences of the past and even the past lives and is motivated, therefore, to carry out such actions that are prompted by past experiences. Present actions again form the base for future thoughts and actions. Thus mind creates past, present and future.

The natural state of mind is stillness. In stillness the three qualities of mind, namely – Sattva, Rajas and Tamas are in equilibrium. When this equilibrium is disturbed Rajasic quality becomes dominant leading to action and consequent experiences. Then, it is necessary to control Rajasic quality and regain the state of equilibrium, the natural state of mind, which is peaceful, calm and serene.

The motivating force for all actions is Divine Will and as such, the results of all actions are also decided by the same. That Divinity in the body is the Self or the individual consciousness.

There are four principal sayings drawn from the four Vedas. They are:

Aham Brahma Asmi	:	**I am the Divine Consciousness, Brahma.**
Tat Tvam Asi	:	**You are also that Divine Consciousness.**
Ayamatma Brahma	:	**All around is that Divine Consciousness Prevailing.**
Prajnanam Brahma	:	**Prajnanam is explained as Brahma.**

Prajnanam is that consciousness that is awake under the three states of existence – wakeful state, dream state and sleep state – and is supervising the functioning of the body. This is the soul or Self.

This pure intelligence, the absolute within, is covered by maya or illusion and is responsible for the creation of a variety of thoughts that originate and die incessantly in the mind. Once the thoughts are controlled and suppressed and mind is made still the Divine nature of the inner self will be revealed. To control mind it is necessary to understand the nature of the mind. Every step in the process of controlling the mind will be vehemently opposed and mind will try to run away from all control that are being imposed on it. Hence, to control this ever escaping mind from control, great courage, strength, intelligence and will power are required.

'I' and 'Mineness' manifest as mind. Now, it is needed to understand the root cause that thinks rather than on the thought. If it is possible to know – who is thinking – and control that source then there will be no thoughts at all. This is "I" that develops possessiveness. The task is difficult only because that attempt is made to understand mind through mind only. There are thoughts so long this "I"-ness exists. If "I" and "Mine" thoughts are eliminated then there will be no more disturbing thoughts that create an illusion on the mind and prevent clear understanding of the nature of the Self. In other words, mind will become a bridge to illuminate the source where the Divine Consciousness or Self dwells.

A first step to realize the Self is to turn the mind inwards by closing the eyes and observe silence. Practicing this with great diligence leads to a situation where the incessant thoughts become lesser and lesser and finally cease to arise. This is all within one's reach. Everyone is entitled to realize that state where there is peaceful, tranquility, and immense happiness. Persistent efforts are needed to sustain this peaceful state as sooner or later thoughts will creep into mind and explode with greater vigor. For this Divine Grace, 'Sadgurus' guidance is necessary. When one struggles constantly praying the lord for such a guidance and when it is genuine that guidance will be made available to him.

The realized state of mind can not be described and has to be experienced by oneself. It can be said that for a person who has controlled his mind every work will be accomplished with ease. Success follows in all his endeavours.

Happiness

Happiness is internal and not external. Yet, man is trying to find happiness in external objects like money, power, name, fame, position and similar such things. He is leading a self centered life. Entering in to an unscrupulous competition to amass wealth he is engulfing himself into worries, disappointments and dejection. Only after experiencing bitter knocks in the routine mundane life, his attention is drawn slowly inwards, seeking solace and rest in the realm of his own spiritual self. Man can realize his inherent state of happiness only when he understands – mind, its operating principles, its nature and ways and means for the control of it. It is the mind by its mercurial wandering and wavering nature, biased by pride and prejudices, likes and dislikes, causes anxiety, produces anger and frustration that finally results in immense stress to the physical body. This has been explained in Gita.

If one dwells in his mind about objectives of sense, an attachment develops in his mind. This attachment gives rise to desire. If the desire is not fulfilled anger materializes. From anger comes delusion. Delusion leads to loss of mental balance which, in turn leads to deprivation of comprehending power. Then one perishes with lack of understanding. Worldly objects do not give permanent satisfaction. All mundane pleasures are transient and ephemeral. According to a 8th century Buddhist monk Santideva "all the joy the world contains has come from wishing happiness to others – all the misery the world contains has come through wanting pleasure for one self". One should investigate into the nature of this phenomenal world and of the mind. The keys to happiness and suffering are to be determined. Once the reason for ignorance is found out realization emerges. All these discoveries contribute to knowledge.

There is divinity in every object of creation. Human life is the highest in evolution. It is said that 8, 40,000 different species are created, the last of which is human form. To give it a meaning for its existence, spiritual endeavor is essential that is pure and holy. Man is absolutely competent to realize his innate divine nature – which is nothing but a state of happiness.

Man and His Spiritual Bodies

A state of well being of the body is concerned with good health in the physical plane, freedom from all sorts of worries and passions in the emotional plane and enjoying a state of tranquility in the mental phase. A total unification of body with soul is the ultimate health index.

The physical body is made up of five basic elements – Ether, Air, Fire, Water and Earth. However for spiritual explanation, bodies with different characteristics are defined, operating in different planes of existence. Thus, there are twenty five components made out of these five basic elements.

Nature followed a systematic procedure to create the twenty five components. Consider Ether or 'Akash' element. One unit of 'Akash' is taken and divided into two halves. Each half is again divided into five equal parts. Then, for example one tenth part of ether with the other one tenth part gives rise to knowledge, one tenth part of Akash with one tenth part of air creates mind, another with one tenth of fire creates intellect. Likewise, with water reflective mind and with earth, ego are produced which constitute the pentad of internal organs. The creation and composition of all the five pentads are given in the table below.

Element	Ether	Air	Fire	Water	Earth	Organs
Ether	Knowledge	Mind	Intellect	Mind stuff	Ego	Internal organs
Air	Circulating (Samana)	Digestive (Vyana)	Transmi-gration (Udana)	Perception (Prana)	Excretion (Apana)	Vital airs
Fire	Ears	Skin	Eyes	Tongue	Nose	Sense organs
Water	Sound	Touch	Sight	Taste or flavor	Smell	Sensations
Earth	Vocal chord	Hands	Legs	Genitals	Anus	Work organs

The physical body is called "Sthula Deha" or "Sthula Sareera" (gross body) in metaphysics. This body is composed of 25 components. They are the following

(a) The five components of vital airs (Panch Pranas).

Prana (perception), Vyana (digestion),

Udana (transmigration), Samana (circulation) and Apana (excretion) air or Vayu.

(b) The five internal sense organs (Antarendriyas) knowledge, mind, intellect, consciousness and egoism (or Jnan, Manas, Buddhi, Chitta and Ahamkara). Chitta can also be called the Reflective mind.

(c) The five sense organs or organs of perception (Jnanendriyas):

Ears, eyes, tongue, nose and skin (ie) Shrota, Chakshu, Jinhva, Nasika and Tvakku.

(d) The five sensations or attributes of Sense Organs (Panch Tanmatras) sound, sight (colour and form), taste or flavour, smell and touch or shabda, rupa, rasa, grandha, sparsa and

(e) the five work organs or ogans of action (karmendriyas)

These are, vocal chord (mouth), hands, legs, anus and genitals – which implement the afferent and efferent impulses to human desires, feelings and emotions.

In vedic parlance, as stated in Taittareyopanishad, the physical body is also called "Annamaya Kosha" meaning the physical sheath that is dependent on food consumed by the person for his existence.

Inside this physical sheath, there is a vital sheath "pranamaya kosha". This is the energy body of a person. Within this prananaya kosha, a mental sheath or "manomaya khosa" is located. This is the body driven by mind and intellect or "Antahkarana". Further, inside the mental sheath is the "vijnanamaya kosha" or the intellectual sheath actuated by buddhi or intellect, the discriminating power.

While the sthula sareera or the physical body has all the 25 components, a subtle body or "Sukshma Sareera", is conceived as comprising of the vital sheath, the mental sheath and the intellectural sheath consisting of only 17 components of the gross body viz – five sense organs, five work organs, and five vital airs along with mind and intellect. This subtle body is also called "astral body" or "linga sareera".

Within the intellectual sheath or "Vijnanamaya kosha" another body called "Anandamaya kosha", karana sareera or "seed body" is present.

It has the attributes of chitta, the reflective mind and pragna – the constant integrated awareness. It is also called casual body. This body is responsible for the cycle of births.

Within the Karana sareera, exists "super casual body" or "mahakarana sareera" which is self luminous and self radiant.

The existence of seed body or karana sareera is attributed to the sequence of actions performed. This is explained further. Ignorance of self leads to egoism. This in turn leads to love and hatred that results in performing various actions. The results of these actions assume human form (birth) to reap the consequences of actions performed-good or bad.

Creation and the Creator

The origin of the universe is shrouded in mystery. Every one agrees that the universe must have some source. A little thinking will always reveal that the creator has to be one that has no comparison. He (or She) has got to be entirely different from everything else that we know in the world. This primal cause of cosmos or the universe is called in Vedas "Brahma", "Iswara", "Atma" and by several other names. This Brahma, the cosmic person, also called God, is the Vaiswanara, or Viswa virat, indicating that he is the individual (consciousness) multiplied by infinity (universal consciousness). This integrated human mind is the cosmic mind and is thus named Hiranya Garbha.

Svaroopabodha upanishad describes Him as an embodiment of self luminous, and illuminating undivided Supreme Lord. He has no attributes. He is stainless, timeless, space less, causeless and cannot be understood through any known method directly.

As expounded in the Jyothirbindu Upanishad, he is all pervading and is the soul of all.

Advaitananda Upanishad asserts that he is the one without the second. He is self contained. He is within and without.

Sivajnanamrita Upanishad describes Him:

"Nirgunam, Nirakaram, Nirvisesham, Akhandam Nirupadhikam Ekamevadviteeyam, Swatantram,Nityamuktam, Paripoornam":

Meaning that the Supreme Lord is

"Attributeless, formless, without any special features without parts, without any limiting adjuncts, one without a second, independent, ever free and all – full".

He is the originator, sustainer, and destroyer of the world. He is the pure intelligence with consciousness that is absolute and transcendental.

Svaroopabodha Upanishad maintains that understanding this Supreme Soul, is attaining the imperishable state of self realization. This attainment is called ' Liberation' or 'Moksha'.

This means that one reaches a stage where he finds his own self staying or resting in its own native state of divine glory.

Eesavasyopanishad says that the whole universe, which manifests in the mind, is only Brahma or Eeswara, the Supreme Lord. This famous upanished exhorts one to lead a simple life. One must perform his daily duties with a sense of sacrifice. It is advised that one should not aspire to possess other's wealth.

Brahma is stated to be static but could be dynamic also. When He manifests in mind or gets associated with any other object, He becomes dynamic. He is very near, but could also be too far. For the realized person He is near and for the ignorant He is far. For those who understand His all pervading nature or omnipresence, there is no scope for attachment or worries. This Brahma, also called Atma is not affected by the fruits of the right or wrong doings of the person.

Realization of this "All–Seer" and absolutely righteous and self luminous "Atma" is made possible through altruistic or self less service and love.

Sun and fire are also considered as the other manifestations of the creative force in the nature and are considered for worship in Vedas. Worshipping the non manifest form of Brahma is considered to lead one to eternal life or liberation of soul.

According to Kenopanishad Brahma is the one who gives life to universal life force that sustains the creation. He is the one that is responsible for the mind to mind its duty. He is the power behind the eyes to posses sight. He is the energy behind the tongue that is able to talk and communicate. He is the power that motivates the ears to hear and respond or comprehend. He is the one called "Paramatma" that stands alone in his own supreme and self luminous glory. This divine glory is not cognized by logic or any other means but can be reached through a teacher or guru. Guru is the one who can dispel the darkness or "Avidya" (ignorance) of the disciple and can lead him into light (enlightenment).

Those who think that they have understood Him have not understood him. Those who think that they have not understood him, have in fact understood him.

This is stated in the Upanishad as follows.

Avijnaatam vijaanataam
Vijnaatam avijaanataam

Any amount of knowledge gained by the study of Vedas, upanishads, or other spiritual scriptures will only purify the mind and centre it towards the goal, but cannot directly take anyone to it.

The self, which is also the source of creation must be realized or understood during one's life time only, since after death nothing can be accomplished. One can move into its nature through constant meditation. Devotion, meditation, prayers etc are means in this direction.

Vedas say that He is the power that controls the wind so that it can blow or not and He ordains the fire to burn and all senses exhibit their characteristics only with His permission.

By realization it is meant that one should experience that the individual soul or self is not different from the cosmic consciousness. In yogic parlance this supreme state is called 'Nirvikalpa Samadhi' (thoughtless super conscious state) or 'Asamprajnata Samadhi' (absolute or highest super conscious state).

Prana - the Vital Force

It has been explained that the gross body contains five vital airs – Prana, Vyana, Udana, Apana and Samana. All the five components together are also referred to as Prana. The functioning of Prana from nose to navel through its five components is explained now.

Prana acting as Vyana (diffused breathing), present in the entire body, affects division and diffusion resisting disintegration and holding all the parts of body together.

The upward moving air is called Udana. While sun is considered as the external manifestation of Prana, Udana that moves up is the internal reflection of it in human body. Body gets cooled if it cannot obtain Tejas (energy) from the sun. Prana component works from nose to navel and is seated at the heart while Apana works down from the navel.

Jeevatma (the embedded soul) or Lingatma (the individual soul) is seated in the heart according to Vedas.

Samana is the component of Prana that gives the essence of food to the body and is located at the navel. Udana is seated at throat. Apana is located at anus. Earth takes Apana while the Sun gives Prana and sight.

Prasnopanishad considered prana – as Mukhya prana (with all its components) as force that controls all the activities in the body. It intends and action follows.

It eats the result of the work done. It ordains the various organs to function properly as explained.

Aitareyopanishad too explained that the indwelling divine force is the vital force or prana. According to this Upanishad, before creation, there was only the non dualistic Supreme Atma existing in the unmanifest form. The first subtle form of the Divine Soul is "Hiranyagarbha", while the manifest form that came up later is called Virat. Virat purusha or vaiswanara, manifested the universe. Hiranyagarbha represents the aggregate of the individual consciousness i.e. the cosmic consciousness. The manifested form is transformed into two. One attracted the other. Thus, from the first progenitors creation started and when the species so created reached the magical 84 lakh number; the last born was human.

As per Prasnopanishad, it was the sun by his relative movement causing day and night produced the concept of time, punctuated by days, months, seasons and year. Natural forces that sustain life along with sun are called Devas or Gods and they entered into the human body to control the activities of the various organs in the body. All the body activities are thus coordinated, controlled and sustained by the vital force or mukhya prana through its various components.

There are astral nerves called "Nadis" in the body. These are 72,000 nadis in human body. In addition to these 72,000 nadies, there is one more important nadi, which is a basic nerve without any branches called "Sushumna" nadi directed upwards along which prana, called udana moves. These nadis were discussed earlier.

In the body, mind is the apparent source of all power. Everything merges there. So, a sleeping person cannot smell, cannot see, cannot perceive, cannot speak, cannot accept anything, cannot participate in anything and so on. But it is the five forms of prana that are awake and performing their respective functions.

God is reflected in every body and every thing. Where there is water sun's rays reflect in water. When water, evaporates, the rays recede back to sun and there is no reflection. So also, after death prana, God's reflection, goes back to him.

Prana is the purusha (the soul) that lives in the 'puri', the city that is the body.

Steps to Self

There are several guidelines pronounced in the scriptures, which must be practiced before any serious attempt is made to realize the soul.

Jyotirbindu Upanishad says that one must control all senses, anger, passion and develop cosmic love, forgiveness, fearlessness and other qualities that will lead to detachment. At the very first thought of seeking liberation one must give up all desires.

In Sankhya system of philosophy, nature is said to be made up of three forces that keep it in equilibrium. They are Sattva, Rajas and Tamas corresponding to the three states of equilibrium, activity and inertness.

In the state of Rajas, mind seeks power and enjoyment while in the state of Sattva, mind is calm and serene. In the Tamas state, there is no activity of the mind and when anything occurs in that state it is only to cause harm to others due to stupidity. Elimination of Rajas and Tamas and enhancement of Sattva is a step in the direction of realization.

Anadabindu Upanishad asserts that realization of atma, the embodiment of happiness can be achieved through observing silence and removing all obstacles in the way. In silence, the distinction between the seer, the sight and the seen are to be eliminated. The "I" concept has to be given up.

Taittareyopanishad in fact, prescribes a code of conduct for those who aspire to understand divinity. It contains:

- Speak the truth always
- Observe the rules that form the law (dharma) as ordained in scriptures
- Respect parents and the teacher
- Take proper care of the body
- Earn money through lawful means
- Give charity with devotion as per your financial status
- Respect the religious scriptures and do not forget whatever is learnt.
- Treat the guests as the divine representatives.

Such a code of conduct will discipline the mind.

Mundakopanishad emphasises the need for understanding the difference between "Truth" and "Untruth", and give up worldly attachments as a prelude to understand the Self. It further states that one should give up the aspiration for post death heavenly pleasures if any.

Yogasaropanishad maintains that through love, mercy, magnanimity, truthfulness, celibacy and other sattvic characteristics and practicing meditation one can realize the Self.

The state of thoughtlessness can be reached by worshipping attributeless atma through altruistic service and realize the self as suggested by Eesavasyopanishad.

Ignorance and Knowledge

Happiness derived from worldly pleasures is called "Preyassu". Performing various rituals and sacrifices through action (karma), it is possible to obtain worldly pleasures.

Through self realization, one can experience the indescribable joy in his own native state of divine consciousness. This happiness is called, "Sreyassu". The former i.e. "Preyassu" is experienced through ignorance, the latter, that is "Sreyassu" is experienced through absolute knowledge called Brahmavidya or knowledge of the Supreme consciousness. Thus, all sacrifices and rituals performed in accordance with the prescribed rules using all the ingredients as required and specified in vedic texts will only give limited benefits which are not permanent. This is explained in Kathopanishad. Plants, insects and animals have no thinking power and discriminative intellect. Their life is guided by the laws of nature. It is only man who can think, discriminate between good and bad and gain knowledge through scriptures and can perform various deeds. Ignorance and knowledge are interwoven and confuse the human mind. He should clearly distinguish and follow the path towards liberation of mind, avoiding, thus, the cycles of birth and death.

The state of self realization is described as perfect control of all desires and complete annihilation of wanderings of even the sub conscious mind. That self which has to be realized is not bounded by any of the limits that exist in nature and is also unchanging with time and is unattached to the results of all actions.

One will understand that the task of seeking the self is infinitely difficult since the self is not seen by the eyes, has no shape and has no organs. The omni present, omniscient is extremely subtle. Atma can be seen as the firmament for all objects that are seen – both animate and inordinate. Mundakopanishad states that Brahma created the whole world from within, just as a spider weaves a cobweb without any external assistance but from within only. Just as hair grows on skin or as grass grows from earth so also, the universe that arises from the Virat Purusha is in a manifest form.

Embodied and Cosmic soul

Self is realized by those who renounce every thing and seek it only. Kathopanishad advises the seeker to give up all bad deeds that harm others and give up attachments that give momentary pleasures. Following the advice of guru, constantly reflecting it in the mind and meditating on it will lead to the desired goal.

It is also desired to give up all benefits that may appear when one reaches the super conscious state. In the normal state the Self, seated in the heart, cannot be perceived due to illusion. All attempts are to be made to get rid of this illusion called maya. The individual soul (Jeevatma) experiences the result of its past actions in the present and will be experiencing the results of his present actions at a later time.

The time period for experiencing the reactions to past actions may extend over several births and deaths for an individual soul. The supreme soul also staying along with the individual soul within the body will only witness the happenings, but will be untouched by them. When the individual soul realizes that it is none other than the cosmic soul or it is not different from it (Brahma), instantaneous release is obtained from all afflictions and becomes one that enjoys the eternal bliss (Jeevanmukta).

Meditation and the Self

Meditation is suggested as the most important means in the endeavor to self realization. **Svaroopabodhoupanishad** and **vedantasaropanishad** advocate constant meditation. Various means are proposed as objects of meditation. The first and foremost is the pranava nada, the primal sound "AUM". There are other great vedic statements on super reality viz.

TAT TVAM ASI - Thou Art That

AHAM BRAHMASMI - I am Brahma (the Cosmic Soul)

PRAJNAANAM BRAHMA - Consciousness is Brahma.

Protracted meditation on the above with right thinking, right action and right conduct – the soul can be realized.

Vicharabinduupanishad emphasizes that profound meditation on "Tattvam Asi" and "Aham Brahmasmi" will lead to the desired destination. Observance of truth, celibacy penance and self restraint are basic preconsiderations for successful meditation. With absolute detachment and renunciation of pleasures and pains and through daily vigorous meditation, self can be realized.

Advaitamruta upanishad endorses that the unchanging pure conscience – self, can be grasped only by overcoming several obstacles with absolute dedication and continuous practice of meditation. One has to break all bonds and identify oneself with everything. Brahmanubhava Upanishad agrees with this, adding further that meditation on the vedic pronouncements – such as Aham Brahmasmi, Tat Tvam Asi, and constant contemplation on "I am the absolute super consciousness", will lead to self realization.

The world exists only in our 'Sankalpa' or imagination. When all thoughts about 'I' are dissolved, a state of tranquility is reached leading to liberation; liberation of self from the veil of thoughts that are created constantly by the mind. The restraint of thoughts will lead to the state of super consciousness. Thought is said to be a dynamic force that arises from chitta, the mind stuff.

Concentration of mind, fixing it on some point, an object – internal or external is considered as a means for self realization. The state so attained is called Samadhi. Protracted meditation with right thinking, right action with right conduct and subdued senses will lead to samadhi state.

Breaking down the various layers of ignorance, identified as different sheaths towards absolute bliss is achieved step by step under the guidance of a guru.

When one understands the principle of 'Advaita' or 'monism' which posits dual aspect of single consciousness – one the transcendental changeless aspect – and the other the creating. changing aspect, then the self is realized.

In meditation one will realize that the spirit or atma is unchanging but its power is active and changes into mind and matter. Due to collective 'Samskaras' or 'Vasanas'. i.e., mental impressions and tendencies produced by actions accomplished in previous births, one will accumulate avidya or ignorance. This veil of ignorance or maya covers the spirit, the ultimate irreducible reality – called also pure consciousness and is thus required to be destroyed through knowledge and meditation.

Pranava – the Universal Sound

The sound AUM is called Pranava. The first letter "A" is the root sound, pronounced without touching any part of the tongue or palate, "U" comes from the root to the end of the sounding board of the mouth. "M" is produced by closing the lips. As such AUM represents the whole phenomena of producing the sound.

Postscript

Indian philosophy is a realistic or practical pathway to attain self realisation. When this self realization happens the influence of dualities ceases. Ignorant men may call it "day – dreaming", but there are infinite instances of people who have reached their goal of this permanent bliss. Staying in that state of happiness, they performed their daily duties efficiently, remaining in this world as part and parcel of it. The secret of such a life is the elimination of "I-ness" and "mine-ness", that is, one must attain freedom from selfishness and attachment. Developing universal love, which means, "seeing self" in all. Indian holy scriptures provide an immense source of knowledge that guides man to lead a happy life in this world and be an ideal universal citizen. Love, sacrifice, selfless service are the corner stones on which Indian moral and philosophic edifice is built.

Vedas (which are immortal and eternal) are the basic building blocks for the Indian civilization and culture.

As has been stated already that the doctrine proclaimed on the basis of Vedas followed by people of India is called 'Sanatana Dharma' which is popularly called Hinduism.

This Dharma or Hinduism has only one point agenda, discussed at length and examined from all points of view and established beyond doubt. It is dealing with the unity of embodied soul of man (Jeevatma) with the universal or cosmic consciousness (Paramatma). From this point, Hinduism is a religion, as religion means – union of self again with its source – or self – realization. The endeavor of all religious scriptures, in fact, is to guide man achieve this unity of human consciousness with the Divine.

Patanjali is Raja – Yoga

Patanjali in his Raja Yoga said" Tasya---------------

"Tasya Vachakah Pranavah" – meaning that the manifesting word for God is AUM. Repetitive use of a mantra (mystically powerful composition of letters or words to be recited for spiritual up liftment) accelerates the spiritual journey.

Narayanopanishad states

"Pratyaganandam Brahmapurusham

Pranawasvaroopam – Akara Ukara Makara Iti"

As emphasized in Sivajnanopanishad, AUM is the symbol of Brahma. From it, the world is projected, in it the world exists and in it is the world involved during cosmic dissolution. It is the essence of Vedas.

Mandukyaupanishad declares that the universe merges in A, power merges in U and consciousness merges in M. **Prasnopanishad** prescribes meditation on AUM as means for reaching the self. The meditation should be in a unified manner with all the three syllables. One should contemplate that – "he is the immortal self, he is the all pervading intelligence", while meditating on AUM. Such a feeling will annihilate the maya or illusion on the mind. A grand sublime exhalted and ineffable state can be realized. This is the suggestion given in Sivajnanamrita Upanishad.

According to **Taittareyopanishad –**

"AUM Iti Brahma

"AUM Itidagum Sarvam"

The sound "AUM" is the symbol of the Supreme Lord. All that is seen is the manifestation of AUM only.

Treat AUM as a bow. Use the embedded soul (Jeevatma) as an arrow. Shoot the arrow with the bow so as to merge the Jeevatma with cosmic consciouness i.e. Paramatma. That is the way Mandukyopanishad opines about meditation on AUM to realize the self.

Mandukyopanishad gives an interesting revelation about meditation on AUM. The soul has four fold personality. The first manifestation of atma is the wakeful state. In this state he enjoys the world with his five sense organs. (sound – ear, touch – skin, sight – eye, taste – tongue and smell – nose). He is then Vaisawanara. The second manifestation of atma is the dream state. In this state atma creates a world of its own, without any external help and lives in it. The third state in which atma manifests is the sleep state. Beyond this sleep state is the fourth state Turiya, the super conscious thoughtless state where Atma dwells.

"Cosmic consciousness, that is God is omnipresent, omnipotent and omniscient.
He is the originator, sustainer and destroyer of the Universe.
He is reached through deep and constant meditation.
Meditation on the primal sound AUM is gateway to self realization."

References

1. Illustrated History [illegible]eligions: Edited by John, Cambridge University Press (2002)
2. Illustrated Dictionary Of Religions, Rituals, Beliefs, and practices around the world: Philip Wilkinson. Dept. of theology and religious Studies, Rochmpton Institute, London.
3. Human Physiology: Expression of Veda and Vedic literature: By Prof. Tony Nadir Ram Maharshi Vedic University
4. Hindu Scriptures: Swamy Shivananda The Divine Life Society, Rishikesh. (U.P)
5. Hindu Scriptures: V.A.K.Aiyar www. Hinduism.co.za/ vedas
6. Hymns of Rigveda: Ralph Griffith, T.H. with a popular commentary in English, 1895
7. Hymns of the Sama veda: Ralph Griffith T.H. translated into English with commentary (1895)
8. The Sama Veda: Sanskrit text with English translation, Devi chand Munshiram Manoharlal Publishers Pvt. Ltd .New Delhi.
9. The Yajurveda: Sanskrit text with English translation. Devi Chand. Munshiram Manoharlal Publishers Pvt. Ltd. New Delhi.
10. The Atharva veda, Sanscrit text with English commentary. Devi chand, Munshiram Manoharlal Publishers pt ltd. New Delhi.
11. The Sama Veda Samhita: Revised and edited by Nag Sharan and Surendra Pratap (1991), Nag Publishers Delhi.
12. The Hymns of the Atharva veda: Ralph Griffith T.H., 1895-96
13. Hymns of the Atharva Veda: Maurice Bloomfield, Sacred Books of the East. Vol 42 (1897)
14. Rigveda: Wikipedia the free encyclopedia
15. Yajurveda: Wikipedia the free encyclopedia
16. Sama Veda: Wikipedia the free encyclopedia
17. Atharva Veda: Wikipedia the free encyclopedia
18. Yajurveda Taittareya Samhita: Arthur Berriedale Keith, English (1914)

19. Aitareya Aranyaka: Arthur B. Keith, Eastern Book Linkers (1995)

20. Rigveda Brahmanas: studies in the Brahmanas, A.C. Banerjea, Motilal Banarsidas (1963)

21. Six Systems of Indian Philosophy [illegible] Mueller (1899), Susil Gupta Calcutta.

22. Philosophies of India: S. Radhakrishnan and moore Princeton University Press, New York.

23. Prajna vilasamu; (Telugu) Dr. P. Jaganmohan Rao Agastya Publications, Hyderabad.The World teacher trust.

24. Aitareyopanishad — Sri Kompalle Dakshinamoothy garu

25. Kathopanishad — Sri Kompalle Dakshinamoothy garu

26. Mundakopanishad — Sri Kompalle Dakshinamoothy garu

27. Eesavasyopanishad — Sri Kompalle Dakshinamoothy garu

28. Prasnopanishad — Sri Kompalle Dakshinamoothy garu

29. Kenopanishad — Sri Kompalle Dakshinamoothy garu

30. Chandogyopanishad — Sri Raayavaram Veereswara Sarma garu

31. Mandukyopanishad — Sri Trivikrama Ramananda Bhrati Swamy garu; Sri Vimalananda Bharati Swamy garu

32. Taittareyopanishad — Sri Kanuparthi Markandeya Sarma garu

33. Brihadaranyopanishad — Sri Suri Koti Sastry garu

All the above 23 to 32 are published by Seetha Rama Adi Sankara Trust, Anand bagh, malkajigiri, Hyderabad in Telugu.

34. An Analysis of Brahma Sutras: www.Sankaracharya.org

35. The Serpent Power: Sir John Woodroffe, Ganesh and Co. Madras.